CW01496755

Bread and Milk

Karolina Ramqvist

Karolina Ramqvist is one of the most influential writers and feminists of her generation in Sweden. She has written five novels prior to *Bread and Milk* and is widely celebrated for her powerful ability to provoke quiet yet fierce questions rather than provide loud and easy answers. In her skilful hands, contemporary issues of sexuality, commercialisation, isolation, and belonging become highly charged and, at the same time, completely unaffected. In 2015 Ramqvist was awarded the prestigious P. O. Enquist Literary Prize for her novel *The White City*. She is also the author of *Bear Woman*.

Saskia Vogel grew up in Los Angeles and currently lives in Berlin, where she works as a writer and Swedish-to-English literary translator. She has written on the themes of gender, power, and sexuality for publications such as *The White Review*, *The Offing*, and *The Quietus*. Previously, she worked as *Granta* magazine's global publicist and as an editor at the AVN Media Network, where she reported on pornography and adult pleasure products. She is the author of the novel *Permission*.

Bread and Milk

Karolina Ramqvist

MANILLA
PRESS

First published in the UK in 2025 by
MANILLA PRESS
An imprint of Zaffre Publishing Group
A Bonnier Books UK company
5th Floor, HYLO, 103–105 Bunhill Row,
London, EC1Y 8LZ
Owned by Bonnier Books
Sveavägen 56, Stockholm, Sweden

Originally published as *Bröd och mjölk* in Sweden in 2022 by Norstedts

A CIP catalogue record for this book is
available from the British Library.

Hardback ISBN: 978-1-78658-331-4

Also available as an ebook

1 3 5 7 9 10 8 6 4 2

Typeset by IDSUK (Data Connection) Ltd
Printed and bound in Great Britain by Clays Ltd, Elcograf S.p.A.

Manilla Press is an imprint of Zaffre Publishing Group
A Bonnier Books UK company
www.bonnierbooks.co.uk

For my family

Food is love. People say so all the time. I hear it ever more often nowadays and I know this to be true. But to me this also meant that love was food.

A former anorexic once said as much to me, many years ago, when I'd invited her along with some other friends over for a meal. My large white dining room table was set with mismatched china and old cutlery of a style that had taken a long time to track down. The table was standing in the middle of the one-room apartment I lived in back then, and she walked over and let her eyes wander across it and everything I had laid out: a thick wedge of Parmesan cheese, a bowl of French string beans, a plate of young green leaves and thinly shaved fennel, roasted artichokes in my mother's white soufflé dish from the 1980s, steamed broccolini with garlic and lemon, and in the middle of it all a deep ceramic dish into which I was about to pour a steaming pot of spaghetti arrabiata with fresh basil leaves and pieces of half-melted buffalo mozzarella.

I had opened two bottles of wine and set out two carafes of water, along with the bread I'd baked in the gas oven that morning and cut into thick slices, so the guests could tear hunks off to eat with olive oil and flaked salt as they settled in at the table.

She took it all in and smiled.

You show your love through food, she said.

I fell silent and dropped my gaze. I couldn't look her in the eye as those words were striking me, but I looked at all the food sitting there, feeling stupid that this had never occurred to me. On some level, of course, it had, but I'd never put the thought into words the way she had, as if she were free to say anything she liked. I for one had never talked to anybody else about my relationship with food and had never articulated it to myself, and I felt ashamed that it could be so obvious to another person.

Thinking about it now, I realize that she simply may have been pointing out how we differed when it came to what is called the language of love – that is, how we show the people we love that we love them.

But it's also possible that she understood.

I imagine she did, because she knew a thing or two about what food can be and how it can be used, and I think her words were what allowed me to get such a clear picture of myself not long thereafter, when I made that rice pudding for my daughter and was confronted with myself, in all my lack and ineptitude.

Everything I couldn't do or say.

I used to think it was right after this incident that I began seeking out others with problems similar to my own, in order to solicit help. But in reality it took much longer. After all, memory is deceptive. It's hard to remember one's life. It's hard to remember in the right order, and as for this matter of food, I don't know how it all began or why.

Those I sought out said it might begin with the very first sustenance. The milk that is so rich and sweet, that satisfies and soothes the newborn child and relieves its pain. We might be wishing for a return, to once more be allowed to drink while resting in someone's arms. One might think it would be easy to speak in terms of 'we,' because we all must eat in order to survive. But people are so varied. I see the love of food everywhere, simple and full of pleasure, and I wonder if there aren't others like me, after all.

T ell my story, they said, it's the only way to get free. It's not that my story is special – they say this to everyone. It's one of their guiding principles; they sound like sober alcoholics when they speak and indeed many of them are – alcoholics and drug addicts who stopped drinking and doing drugs and started on food instead.

But I don't know how to tell the story of what food has meant to me. I'm frightened that I might not have a language for it. I don't believe this story will set me free in the way that they insist they have been set free, and I don't want to turn this into a good story.

Do it anyway, they say.

So I try.

I see before me a tangerine.

This is the beginning. The tangerines. It was winter, citrus season, I think I was three years old. It was the middle of the day and bright outside and the fruits had been set out on the big white table. There may have been thirteen of them, maybe more, but thirteen is the number I haven't been able to get out of my head ever since, and they were bright orange and luminous amidst all the white in our kitchen.

I was alone in there, on the floor by the table, and it was quiet in the apartment. My mother was in her room, working as usual, as she would do on weekends unless one of her friends came out our way for a coffee or a walk around the nearby lake. I remember that I climbed onto one of the chairs and leaned across the white tabletop, reached out and grabbed hold of a tangerine, then picked it up and held it in my hand.

I pressed my nose to it and inhaled its scent, letting the tip of my tongue slip out and over the smooth rind. The bitterness made my tongue retreat, like a small animal into its den. Then I dug my nails into the rind and felt the release of a tangy mist.

I poked a small hole in the rind so I could touch the bare, juicy fruit beneath, then tore off a long strip. Then another and another. When all the peel was discarded, I removed two segments. I thought about how they reminded me of my lips when pressed together. I spread them, scraped away the soft net-like pith, placed one segment between my teeth, and bit down. Juice gushed out, cool and fresh and quenching. And its sweetness filled more than my mouth – it filled the whole of me and the kitchen in which I sat.

I chewed and swallowed and stuffed the other segment in and bit into it as well, felt the fibres in the flesh with my tongue, probed the membranes with its tip for what was still to be had and sucked it into me before I took another segment, doing the same with it and then one more. I was taking the time to chew, but still the juice caught on the way down and it made me cough and clear my throat, but I was undeterred, and once I'd finished the first tangerine, I reached across the big white table for another.

Something new and unknown was racing through me, trembling and burning. I ate one after the next, and when all the tangerines were gone, the sensation vanished as quickly as it had appeared, and it was as if something colourless and slack came over me. I stared at the table, which looked so different now with that untidy heap of rind in place of what had moments ago been plump fruit, full of promise. My fingers were sticky, and vibrant citrus notes rose up around me. I was still on my own in the kitchen. I'd taken a tangerine and tasted it, and then I'd eaten them all up at once. I had done this, me, and yet I could hardly believe it had happened.

—

On the other side of the apartment, I could hear the door to my mother's room opening. I gathered up the peels as quickly as I could and climbed down from the chair to try to dispose of them. She had looked so happy coming home with her bag of groceries. She'd said that tangerines were part of winter, and she was sure I'd like them. A scrap of rind hit the floor, and when I turned around I saw that others had fallen from my hands – hands that were too small to hold everything.

Mom came into the kitchen with her mug of tea. She always drank tea when she was at home. What have you done? she asked. I didn't know what to say, I was just trying to get rid of the tangerine peels that lay like a trail behind me on the floor. Have you eaten all the tangerines?

I couldn't respond.

She looked at me, and when I didn't speak, she bent down and picked up the peels, threw them in the trash, then walked over to the teapot on the counter to refill her mug.

—

I left the kitchen and went into my room to play with my tea tins. If you opened the lids and stuck your nose in, they still contained the aroma of the leaves: jasmine, lemon, muscatel, and osmanthus. She'd taught me all the scents and words, and this was something she seemed to enjoy, but I also noticed that she didn't like that I could smell certain things so clearly and the effect this had on me, how a smell that didn't bother anyone else could drive me to despair.

I put the tea tins in a row on the floor, picked them back up, and built a wall and then a tower. After a while I started to feel itchy. My legs, my inner thighs, prickled and stung, and when I pulled off my thick tights to get at it, I saw that big reddish blotches had spread across my skin. My nails left long white scratch marks. Scratching felt good, but the more I scratched, the worse it got; I felt it on my neck too, my forearms and hands.

I pulled off my shirt so I was sitting in only my underpants; I kept scratching and the itch got worse. When I couldn't stand it anymore and didn't know what else to do, I ran into the corridor outside my room, through the hall, to my mother's room, even though I knew I wasn't supposed to bother her. I walked across the thick white carpet to the other side of the room. She was hunched over her desk, the typewriter and all of her papers next to a plate, empty but for a few rusk crumbs, and the mug, its interior dark with tea. Mama, I said, and she hmmed in reply without looking up from her work. I stood in front of her and started crying, or just let the tears come, to get her attention and to make clear that I had a reason for disturbing her writing time.

She spun around on the chair and looked at me, horrified at the sight of the rash, and then she stood up. Her special scent and warmth enveloped me as she lifted me onto her bed and sat down beside me. I loved her every smell. They were most exquisite in winter, when mixed with the cold. I longed for them always – leather, cigarette smoke, the perfume clinging to her wolf fur when she came to pick me up, and the smell of her skin and body when she was just at home, sitting still or walking around. I looked at the two of us in the mirror beside the desk, like she looked at herself each time before she went out. What is this? she asked, her voice different, unsteady, and a touch shrill rather than deep and soft. What have you done? She stared at the rash, and I remember thinking that I was leaving my body, that I too was looking at myself from the outside, just like she was.

She felt my forehead and said I had a fever and then she picked the large, heavy phone up off the floor, and as she set it on her lap, it emitted a soft metallic ping. She took one of the phone books from the pile under her nightstand, put it next to her on the bed, flipped to a number, and dialled. Then she sat next to me with the receiver in her hand, the phone in her lap, and the long cord winding down her bare legs, her warm freckled skin and her scent, which was like a room of its own that I wanted to find my way into and never leave. She'd been working all morning in the big T-shirt she usually slept in, not having managed to get dressed properly. She had another job too; what she did on the weekends was a side hustle. A bread job, she'd call it.

I squirmed in the bedsheets while she spoke with the person on the other end of the line who was asking questions and of whom she was asking questions in return: How had it happened, was it dangerous, what could be done? When she'd hung up, she went to the kitchen to fetch a tube of ointment she said was in the medicine drawer in the broom closet. She came back with it in hand and squeezed some out, and after she had smeared it into my itchy patches, she stroked my hair and sang to me until I fell asleep.

—

Thinking about it now, I can't remember her being mad at me for eating all the tangerines and bringing hives and an allergic reaction upon myself. What I do remember is the taste, the sweetness in my mouth and how it overtook me. I think it was the first time something I ate transformed me, but I can't say for sure. This is only a memory, the first that arises when I try to look back. And I know memories are not reliable. They belong only to you, and they are only memories, like flashes and echoes through time, images and scenes that further distort each time we call them up.

That big white table is a table meant for a large family, for dinners with many guests, but I have most often sat at it alone. It's a dining room table, but we didn't have a dining room at the time, nor do I have one now. It's in my living room, those eight white chairs arranged around it just like back then. By now two of them have broken, and there's one small mark on the tabletop, as if from the impact of something heavy falling there, but otherwise it looks exactly as it did back then, as when I was a child.

My mother had brought it with her when she left my father, soon after she gave birth to me. It stood in front of the window in our kitchen, which was long, narrow, and dark, and where I'd eat my breakfast each morning. On the white-painted wall above the table, she had put up a large poster of vegetables on a table. In this photographic still life, they were bathed in light, outlines shimmering, so very real and also beautiful. There were pumpkins of various kinds, I remember, and black salsify and beets and a big shiny head of cabbage, whose compressed leaves had veins like the ones protruding from my own skin.

The wall across from it was bare; in the middle was the window, and through the half-open blinds one could see the narrow street and the playground, the cars and buildings, all in the same grey-textured concrete that would glisten when met by sunlight. I saw the brown thorn bushes outside the window, and at the mere thought of putting one of those leaves in my mouth, I'd sense their acidity on my tongue. My maternal grandmother had shown me how to pinch them off and chew them. She was also the one who had pointed out the chervil growing in large clumps at the back of the building, their licorice flavour reminiscent of the gum wrappers I used to pick up from the ground and sniff. Grandma had told me where the rosehips grew and where small, hard apples could still be found, left over from a time before the rental apartments had been built. She pointed out the white nettles jutting from cracks in the asphalt and showed me how to pull off a pedicel and suck down the sweet nectar. Sometimes the nettles were covered in dust from the cars that drove right past them, but the white flowers always seemed untouched, protected by their leaves.

~

The thorn bushes had probably been planted in front of our windows as a form of burglar-proofing. There was talk of building patios for those of us who lived on the ground floor, and I think we dreamed of it happening, of sitting outside on our own patch of earth. But the idea was unlikely to move forward and being out there sounded a bit unsafe, compared to sitting in the kitchen's dining area. There I was protected while still having an overview of the action outside.

In the mornings, the people out there were mostly on their way to school or work. The childminders with their charges all in a row holding on to the same rope, the mothers and fathers, the people who worked in the factory down the way from our building or in offices in the city. A few shift workers on the way home. I remember eating white polar flatbread with light margarine or rounds of dark sour rye bread called rallarhalvor, for breakfast. My mother and Grandma and Grandad had told me about rallare, navvies, that they were the people who had laid the tracks when the railroad was first built, and the rallarhalvor were so stiff and hard around the edges that your mouth stung if you ate too many. I drank the milk slowly and ate the bread in very small bites, making patterns I had plotted out in advance. I looked at where my baby teeth had bitten and imagined arch opening onto arch, one right after another.

~

Light margarine was a staple in our home because butter was bad; my mother didn't like butter and neither did I. She often talked about all the food she didn't like and hadn't been able to eat as a child and about food she still couldn't even bear to smell: fatty foods from the rural southern parts of the country where she grew up, made for people who spent the day working the farm or who came from families that once had done so and maintained this diet out of old habit and because they liked it, pork dripping with grease or breaded fried fish with tiny bones that tickled your throat because it was hard to clean them all away, mash drizzled with melted butter, and fittamad, which she described as a slice of bread spread thick with lard.

I didn't like fatty foods either, and hearing her talk about what meals were like when she was a child made me gag. I loathed cream and butter and meat and was only able to drink extra-skimmed milk, the milk with the lowest fat content that had a bluish tinge on the surface and left no trace in the glass. I had skimmed milk at every breakfast, and while drinking and eating I'd read the back of the milk carton. At first I just looked at the black letters running across the carton's waxed surface, the same lines of characters as were on the tea tins in my room, but as I started to notice them in other places, I made an effort to decipher them – there was an F, an L, an M, a P; my mother liked that I was doing this and explained what the letters sounded like when they were on their own or side by side.

I read the bread bag and the packet of light margarine and the newspaper spread out in front of her, which left black marks on the table that she'd have to wipe away. She sounded happy while she was helping me and I heard her tell others that I was in the process of learning, and one day when she set the milk carton down in front of me on the table, I could see everything that was written there. It was a short piece about the work of a dairy farmer, about how farmers made cream and butter from the milk and how cows kept our landscapes open by grazing in the meadows. It had never occurred to me that this was their doing. I'd seen meadows so I knew meadows existed, but I'd never considered that something had to be done in order to make them look that way.

~

The light margarine went on the smooth dark underside of the polar bread, because it could be spread more thinly there, plus that side had a special flavour – from the baking process as well as the dusting of flour – which was brought out by the margarine. If I ate it plain, I would hold the flat semicircle in both hands and bite off large chunks in a way that made me feel like a child in need. A hungry child being given bread, in a fairy tale or in a program on television.

But one morning when I walked into the kitchen, my mother told me we were out of bread and milk. I wasn't sure what had happened. Had she forgotten to go shopping or not had time because she was late from work or was it something else? Nevertheless, it frightened me that we were out of both, that a pattern could be broken so easily. There had been times when the milk in the fridge had turned sour with lumps that quivered like jelly when poured out, and I'd also known the bread to go mouldy in the bag, not the tangy rallarhalvor but the white bread; it could develop patches of greenish-white spores that let off a stench and left me spitting in the garbage bag after throwing it away.

But not having anything at home was a first. My mother opened one of the freezer compartments and rummaged around for an orange juice she thought she had stashed away. When she couldn't find it, she stood there, staring into space for a moment. Then she opened the fridge and took out the currant cordial from Grandma and Grandad, poured a splash into my glass and diluted it with water, and placed it in front of me. Then she set a cinnamon bun down and told me not to tell anyone what I'd had for breakfast.

The bun was hot and soft with sugar on top and its aroma reached my nose immediately. Yet somehow it looked unsettling there, and I finished it off in only a few bites, unable to take the time to savour this exception. It wasn't nearly as good as I thought it would be either, having the sweet drink as well as the bun in the morning was almost too much; it was nothing like eating the bun with a glass of cold milk like I usually did. When I'd finished eating, she told me to take extra care while brushing my teeth and then we got ready as normal, in silence, and as we left the flat, passed through the gate, and out of the house, I tried to shrink even as I was by her side, holding her hand; I didn't want anyone to notice me.

She brought me to nursery as usual and then I went around my group's room all day wondering what would happen if anyone found out. I was scared but also wanted so badly to tell someone about it. I knew I couldn't. There was good food and there was bad food, and food that was good and desirable in one context could be bad in another. Having cordial and a cinnamon bun for breakfast on an ordinary day was extreme, that much was clear. It went against everything I knew about how days were supposed to unfold, so of course I couldn't discuss it with anyone. I understood, or at least sensed, what my mother had implied: this could be taken as a troubling sign.

—

She had not yet turned forty at that time. I think she was thirty-eight. She had taken the bun from the freezer and defrosted it on a rack in the oven. It had been baked by her mother. Grandma had also had children late, but for reasons other than that she, as a mother, first wanted to do what she'd refer to as her own things. Grandma and Grandad were old and lived far away from us, but if Mom had to go on a trip or do something else or if I got sick and had to stay home from nursery or school, they would jump on the train right away to come help her. And even if I didn't want my mother to disappear, as she would sometimes do, I longed for their visits.

Before they arrived, my mother would go out and buy a certain crisp bread made from rye that my grandfather thought tasted like the kind he'd eaten as a child and that was not available in the shops where they lived. I liked seeing the big packet of crisp bread waiting for him in the cupboard above the fridge and how happy the sight of it made him, though he must have known it would be there or that he could just as easily go out and buy it himself if Mom hadn't had the time.

He'd look so excited when he tore open the packaging with its white paper lining and drew the smell of the rye bread into his big nose. I loved how he and Grandma occupied our apartment with their habits that were so unlike ours. When I came home and opened the door to our building, the smell of cinnamon buns baking would rise like a wall of warmth in the entryway, confirming their arrival. I remember how the days differed when they were with us; it was as if the days gained colour and were filled in a way that sealed off any echoing expanses and voids, and it felt like something good was always happening or about to happen. Every night they made their beds on Mom's corner sofa in the living room and in the mornings they'd tidy it all away again. Our rooms were transformed by their small talk, by radio programs that were always playing, and the smell of spices we didn't otherwise have, like dill seed and caraway and nutmeg that Grandma grated a pinch of on the grater and would sprinkle over our creamy macaroni or add to mashed potatoes.

When she wasn't talking, she was singing her old-fashioned songs about falling in love and the countryside and unhappy love, and he told funny stories about when he worked as an errand boy in the city, at the French brasserie that is still there today, one hundred years later, and that I frequent. My grandfather was still alive when I started going there, but I never thought to tell him. Or did I not want to? I didn't mention that I went there often and had more than once walked from the part of the restaurant where the entrance was in his day to the newer section through the kitchen, where the floor was slippery under my high-heeled shoes and where I knew he had been scolded and slapped by the chef and various cooks for being a minute late or having brought a little too little cheese from the cheese shop that in those days was on the square a few blocks away. Or perhaps they had simply felt like hitting an orphan boy from the countryside who didn't know a soul. Everything that had happened in this restaurant, or in the cheese shop, the sausage shop, and on the surrounding streets, he turned into entertainment. If I was lucky, he would sit me down next to him and show me how the slap would ring in his ears and mimicked the scolding cooks. It was like a performance just for me. I followed every note in his voice and every movement of his face, hoping he would get to the scary part, about the men he had to watch out for on the way home. Even that was a kind of joke, leaving me gasping and with the chills.

—

Grandma used to bring her baking recipes from home, lined A4 sheets that were yellowed and stained with batter and cooking grease, so she could bake mocha squares and coconut macaroons too, but she'd set to work on the wheat dough first. Before putting out the freshly baked buns, she'd pour me a glass of ice-cold milk from the fridge. She'd sit down and watch me eat, and I remember thinking that it was like she and her buns became one.

When I thought of her, I thought of the buns, and vice versa. If I was alone, I'd eat them in a special way so they wouldn't be finished as quickly, even though they were never as good as when she'd just pulled them from the oven and sat down with me and had one herself. I started with the pearl sugar she sprinkled on top, nibbling each pearl off, one by one, with my front teeth until they were all gone and had left barely perceptible holes on the shiny golden surface. Then I grabbed the end bit that jutted out, tore at it, and unspiralled the bun, turning it into a long strip, golden brown at the surface and with raisins or currants baked in and a smattering of cinnamon on the pale, slightly moist sides, and then I ate it. The only time I didn't like her buns was when, instead of raisins, she put diced candied citrus peel in the dough, small rubbery green bits that shocked me with their pungent slipperiness and would continue to disgust me later, each time I saw them in the pantry, like sweet boogers in small clear plastic packages. She swore never to do it again. I'm baking for you, after all, she said, stroking my cheek with her thumb, which would scratch my skin a little at the end. She wanted to know exactly what I liked, so she could make more of it.

Except for the tiny callus at her thumb's cuticle, my grandmother's body was perfectly soft, and when she put me in her lap and held me in her arms, I'd nestle against her belly, her breasts like two large pillows at my back. I could make out the liquids from the dough and ground cardamom on her skin, rose and Fünf Kräuter lozenges on her breath. Her scent was different from my mother's, lighter but almost as complex and intoxicating, and from her clothes came those coarse, caramel-like notes from the body that I could never get enough of.

I sat on her lap and inhaled these scents, caressing her arms and cheeks, the freckles and liver spots and irregularities in the skin, aimlessly and with a sense that all of this was a country of its own, belonging only to me and that only I could see. Her face was full of the same wrinkles and marks; shades of anticipation and delight played across it, along with a hint of a smile around her mouth. As I took her in, her face revealed gratitude and something full-hearted and dreamy, and it seemed as if her gaze were always directed at me, as if she were simply waiting for my wish or for what I was going to say or do, so she could engage.

When she and Grandad were with us, other adults rarely came to visit. There were no dinners and no parties and never anything I had to go to with my mother because I couldn't be anywhere else. We were at home, it was just the four of us or the two of them and me if Mom had gone out, and I never wanted them to go back home.

The last thing she'd do before they left was bake more buns, three trays that she divided up into plastic bags and put in the freezer for us to have when she was gone. She usually went around in her housecoat, brown-speckled and synthetic, a pair of oat-coloured nylon tights that had a tendency to bunch, so she had to bend over, lift up her skirt, and pull them up at the gusset, but when they went to catch the train, she'd wear trousers and a jumper, as she called it, so if I'd forgotten that they were about to leave, I'd be reminded when I woke up in the morning and saw her outfit. I'd never find her still in bed when I got up – she was an early riser, awake long before me or anyone else, even if she was only going to putter around the house all day.

~

Once when they were about to leave, I decided to tell my grandmother how much I would miss her. I thought long and hard about what to say before I plucked up the courage and asked if they couldn't stay. She pulled me onto her lap where she sat on one of the chairs at the big white table, which looked extra white beside her. She wrapped her arms around me and said it wasn't possible, but she would have liked to and they'd be back soon. Then she leaned over and patted the freezer and told me not to forget there were buns in there for me. If I started missing her too much, all I had to do was eat one.

She returned me to the floor and said she would make a rice pudding too, for us to have after she left. Imagine reaching this ripe old age, she said, rocking back and forth on her chair to gain enough momentum to stand up. She often said that. She needed the momentum to get up, and once she was on her feet, she'd let one out almost every time. At least that's how I remember it. I remember thinking it seemed like her bowels would get moving too after she stood up or walked in and out of the kitchen after having been seated awhile, and when the wind made a noise she'd give a bright, almost girlish little cry, as if to camouflage the sound, and sometimes she'd put one hand on her bottom as if to try to stop it. Often another would follow right after, or several in quick succession, giving her no time to drown them out, and then she'd laugh a little and straighten her back and give me an apologetic smile. Other times there came a low blowing sound like when you squeeze out the dregs of a ketchup bottle, so faint that I knew she couldn't hear it herself, but to me it was one of the many signs that she was there with me.

~

When Grandma said the words *rice pudding*, it sounded like she was talking about a secret that only she and I and Grandad were privy to. This was shortly after I'd eaten it for the first time and discovered how delicious it was, and I could also hear a note of laughter in her voice, as if it pleased her that I had begun to like rice pudding as much as she and Grandad did. That I had learned to love a dish that belonged to them.

She complained that we didn't have a proper long pan and would make a double batch using whatever baking pans she could find, so that we could eat rice pudding for days after she left. With butter on top, she told Mom. But Mom wouldn't have any, so there was plenty for me, and she never added any butter. When I was given Grandma's rice pudding for dinner instead of our usual fare, it was like I could transport myself all the way to her and Grandad and the dinette in their apartment where I'd tasted this pudding for the first time – and still it wasn't the same as eating it with them in their home.

The rice pudding was in the fridge, and next to the bags of cinnamon buns in our freezer she had placed her small baked goods, stacked between sheets of waxed paper, in large plastic containers with red wire snap lids she had brought with her. She had to bring with her most of the things she needed for baking because we didn't have them in our kitchen and she didn't want to waste time going to the shops once she'd finally arrived. Maybe she didn't know where to go or how to get there. My teeth ached as I bit through the deep-frozen coffee glaze on her mocha squares and felt the tiny ice crystals in my mouth. I sat on the floor in front of the big white table or under the kitchen counter, in the space next to the refrigerator where a dishwasher was probably meant to go. We didn't have one, as we never had many dishes. It was just the two of us, and we, or I, mostly ate meals that didn't require many pots and pans. On the linoleum floor in the space for the dishwasher was a spot where the heat rose up from the boiler room down in the basement, or maybe it was the drying room in the communal laundry area, and there was the freezer's constant dull hum.

If my mother was home, I ate quickly and quietly, trying to swallow everything down before she came into the kitchen and saw me there, sticky and with crumbs around my mouth; if she wasn't home, I ate slowly, drawing it out as long as possible in the time that I was alone. She was always surprised by how quickly the buns in the freezer disappeared, but when she asked me about it, I had nothing to say. Even if I had wanted to, I couldn't open my mouth and talk to her about it.

It was as if I had swallowed the words along with the rest. I was silent, as was the kitchen, but when I ate something delicious, everything seemed to come alive, inside me and out, and when I'd finished everything, I'd search for more to eat. I scaled the handles of the kitchen drawers to the kitchen counter and opened the cupboards and reached up to feel around the high shelves for a packet of raisins that Grandma might have left behind, or some of the biscuits and rusks that Mom had on her free days when she sat around reading newspapers and drinking tea while nibbling on a little something. I remember thinking that it was as if she were encased, as if a membrane had been drawn around her being, making her impossible to reach.

At my grandmother's house, rice pudding was served in a bone-white earthenware dish with a brown-leaf trim that her mother had passed down to her, not when she left home but later, when she was married and had a family and a home of her own after so many years of working in other people's. It was before the war, as she and Grandad would say, as if there'd only been one war, although they had lived through two and had seen many more play out from afar, and it was before ordinary people like them began to view having a family as a question of love and self-fulfillment.

Throughout those childhood years when I couldn't even imagine tasting her rice pudding, it was probably the hot raisins that put me off, along with the buttery smell that wafted through Grandma and Grandad's dinette. The intrusive yellow of the butter between the white grains of rice, to which Grandma would add an extra knob. Won't you have a taste anyway? she'd ask each time, and I'd squeeze my mouth shut and fix my gaze on the plate, before letting it drift out into the room.

It was a bit dusky in there, even on days when the sun was shining outside. There was a special aroma, a mix of lingering cooking smells, dust, and something stale. On the walls of the dinette were porcelain plates with motifs from around the country and pennants with their political party's symbol nailed to the wallpaper. There were many objects, sounds, and smells that differed from those in our home, and their entire apartment was unlike ours.

Grandma would insist and keep trying, and it was almost as if she'd become a bit stern and her face would stiffen, but when I persisted in shaking my head and pressing my lips shut, she'd eventually place a crisp bread sandwich with the thinnest spread of butter on my plate, and I'd eat it and maybe another just like it while Grandad talked about how good the rice pudding was and what it was like when he and Grandma were kids, back when you had to eat what you were served because you never knew when you'd get your next meal.

That time was like a mayhem that lay behind them. I thought about it often. It was something only the two of them knew about, which they seemed to have only narrowly escaped even though they were now old and so many years had passed. They had been children during the famine of the First World War, when no food had been stored because the authorities were so sure the war would be a short one, meanwhile there were two consecutive years of crop failures and poor harvests.

Our country was now one of the richest in the world, but at that time it had been among the poorest. And it wasn't just that my grandparents had to eat whatever they were given, no matter what, it was everything else on top of it. The violence and the poverty and the disease, being beaten at school, their siblings and parents getting sick and dying, and having to leave home and find work even though they were still just children.

Grandma would usually smile and look straight ahead when Grandad said that. Yes, she'd say, those were mad times, and then it was as if those times would come to life inside of her anyway, her gaze turned inward for a moment before she gave a laugh and looked around as if she didn't know where she was, as if she still wasn't used to the hot food on the table, the carrots and the dishes and the napkin box and the dainty cutlery with black Bakelite handles and everything else in the dim room, and couldn't quite believe it was all real. The sky through the window and the other high-rises lined up along the road.

In my mind, those times were in black and white. I kept trying to get my grandparents to tell me more, to feed my images of what it had been like when they were as young as I was. It was so strange to think that they ever had been. And that everything in those times was so different from the life I was leading that it seemed intangible, impossible to reach from where we were now. Usually Grandad didn't say much more than that children used to have to eat what they were served. The food was there to hush your mouth and you had to make sure there was enough for everyone and maybe sometimes offer up your portion to someone who needed it more or was hungrier than you happened to be. He didn't sound angry when he said this; it was more like an observation about how different everything was now compared to how it was then.

Grandma was more talkative, or so it seemed. In fact, I think she mostly repeated the same stories. Mostly she talked about her mother's childbirths, how she had been present for the births of her younger sisters. I never heard her discuss this with anyone else, but she seemed to enjoy telling me about it. It would begin with a knock at the door and a fine lady walking in and telling her to boil water on the stove and take out some clean towels and rags. That's how Grandma knew the baby was coming, she said, and she had to do it the same way each time. I remember thinking it was strange that she was made to boil the water, her being so young. When that had been prepared, she had to sit on a stool at the far end of the room and wait, at the ready. In the meantime, she could hear her mother, her wailing and moaning, and the lady talking to her, and then there was great relief when the baby came out, brand new and alive and warm. A relief to wipe it off and look closely at its little face, all its fingers and toes, see it searching for the breast and drinking down the milk.

All girls, but no one was disappointed, Grandma said, and I could tell she was proud of her parents for not lamenting the absence of a son. The other story she told began with her asking if I knew that kids in those days had only one pair of shoes. No, I said each time, I didn't, and then she'd tell me that in the summertime all children went barefoot and if the shoes they wore in winter needed mending, her father would make a pair out of newspaper stuffed with straw so they could walk to school. Just think, people used to walk around in paper shoes, she said, shaking her head and putting a morsel in her mouth that she started chew, and I could see those little newspaper shoes in front of me, the lines of text, the pictures I imagined might be in a newspaper in those days and how in the rain or snow she'd run all the way to school in those shoes to try to keep them from falling apart in the wetness.

But the most special story was about an event that took place in the summer of her twelfth year. There had been a thunderstorm, the sky had filled with clouds and turned black, and after it passed, as she was walking home from school, she caught sight of something she'd never seen before: a large orb rolling slowly along the road a short distance away. It turned and headed for her. I could see it in front of me as she spoke, the empty country road, scrawny little Grandma running her heart out to get away, barefoot with her braids dancing across her back. And the orb in pursuit. As she told the story, she'd gesture with her hands to show how big it was, saying she smelled like burning when she arrived home and her mother had said it was a ball of thunder, a globe of energy that can take shape when lightning strikes. It's lucky I didn't let it touch me, she said, but I suppose I could tell it was dangerous.

—

Grandad would say he couldn't remember anything when I'd ask him to tell me about his childhood with his parents and all his siblings. I believe there were ten in total. There was nothing to remember, he said. No, fie on how people lived in those days, Grandma would say, shaking her head. And then she'd fling out her arms: But that's just the way it was! We didn't know any different!

Hearing her say that only made me want to find out more. It was strange how far the life they'd lived as children was from the one we were living in the apartment, where everything was solid and tangible instead of disjointed and unclear, as it seemed to have been then. And somehow I'd get Grandad to say a few things. If he talked, he did so in that tone of voice that suggested a funny story, and afterwards he'd clap the air as if to break the spell it had cast on me. So, he exclaimed, that's enough now! And then he'd give a small shrug over on his chair as if to shake off the last of those times. Hmming, he'd cross one leg over the other and pick his newspaper back up. I felt guilty for wanting to draw it all out of them and for how I longed for it. I was indebted to him and to my grandmother in a way that could never be repaid. I felt for them as I felt for children who had known war – kids I was friends with or had read about and seen on television, children who were given only a little rice or bread to eat because they lived in the midst of war or what war could give rise to – and sometimes I'd limit myself to only a small portion of rice for dinner, to find out what it was like, if it was possible to inhabit another person by eating what they ate.

So it was with the big white table as it is with so many other things that get handed down in a family – I hadn't realized it would one day be mine. I was surprised when my mother asked me if I wanted it, and happy, because it made me think I'd finally grown up. I must have if I had a table like that, right? An expensive piece of high-quality furniture, conceived by a famous designer.

My daughter was only small at the time and we lived in an apartment with an extra room that could be used as a dining room, with enough space for the table and all its chairs. We'd often eat dinner in there and breakfast in the kitchen, at a rickety little drop-leaf table I'd bought at a flea market for my first apartment. In the morning she and I were the only ones awake; I was also the one who did all the shopping and cooking, and every morning I made porridge for her with white quinoa that I'd bought cheaply in a shop that sold Latin American foods.

The kitchen had a pantry so large you could walk right in, with floor-to-ceiling shelves. I'd trimmed the shelves, just like my grandmother had done to her cabinets, using a narrow ribbon that I affixed with white tacks, not coloured ones like my grandmother's, and I took pleasure in arranging the pantry so it looked like a picture in an interior design magazine or one of my cookbooks. Standing there measuring out the quinoa, I'd invariably think of a man I'd met at a party who dealt in quinoa and told me it was easier to bring cocaine into Europe than a new grain that was not a grain but rather an herb and a seed that no one knew how to process. I was recently reminded of this, upon reading that so much quinoa is now being exported from the Andes that the local supply is running out and growers have to eat fast food instead. But I've also heard that this is a myth.

Every morning I rinsed and cleaned the quinoa and let it simmer on the stove with a stick of cinnamon, and at the end I grated in half an apple and added some hazelnuts that I roasted in a pan and peeled by rubbing them together inside a kitchen towel. Considering what my life was like then, my having done this seems so strange. I was a young mother and pretty much the sole breadwinner; I had three jobs, all of which paid too little, and a relationship I couldn't extricate myself from even though I wanted to because I hadn't yet learned how to tell another human being what I wanted and, more importantly, what I didn't want.

But every day I got up and made that porridge. Not doing it was a physical impossibility. She was my first child and I wanted her to feel how much I loved her, so I gave her the best breakfast I could imagine. I loved making the porridge, filling it into her little bowl, quinoa seeds like thousands of tiny Cs, and dusting it with cinnamon. It was as if the suffocating feeling of being stuck that I awoke with each morning dissipated as soon as I went into the kitchen and opened the pantry and started gathering everything I needed. The smell of cinnamon and the white juice of the apple as I grated it. The crunch of the pale nuts as I split them with the kitchen knife and rubbed them together, their shape and hue. The rhythm of it all coming together.

When the porridge was ready, I would set it down in front of her and pour over it almond milk from the fridge to cool it for her. Then I'd sit down and watch as she stuck in her spoon and stirred it around a bit before putting it in her mouth, and then did so again and again, moving her hand up and down, slurping and swallowing. It gave me the same feeling as when she was a newborn and I'd look down at her in my arms, drinking down the milk from my breasts; the satisfaction of seeing her have breakfast was almost as potent, although the feeling that she wouldn't survive if she didn't eat had gone.

—

To the porridge, I often added raisins, which would grow hot and swollen and sometimes disintegrated after boiling for so long. But back then I didn't consider where that addition came from. I was devoted to that action and to the cooking and to everything else in that home because I took pleasure in it and was somehow drawn to it, despite everything else I had to bear. I felt like a hunter and gatherer as I let my eyes roam the shelves of the grocery store and my pantry. Shopping, cooking, and eating food seemed to put me in touch with a populated sphere that had always existed and was different from the one I was in. It gave me a break from everything else, my own thoughts and everything I felt inside and everything I had to do.

With food, it seemed, I didn't have to be anyone or accomplish anything. I could simply be a mouth and a pair of hands, a hole to fill, a rhythm. It was like a secret affair I had begun long before but which intensified in those years when my daughter was young and I was still living with her father. I couldn't tell him how I felt because I was so afraid he'd be disappointed. Every morning I tried to force myself to open my mouth and say that I didn't want this anymore, and some days when I was at work I'd call to check if he was out of the house, then I'd stop what I was doing, go home, sit in the kitchen, and eat.

I'd tended to the household voluntarily and of my own initiative because I thought it was fun, because food was important to me, and because I wanted to make sure that I had certain foods at home and that others were kept away. But if I ever did ask him to go shopping or cook, he'd say he wasn't hungry and therefore wasn't going to do it.

I envied him so for that, for not needing to eat, and for everything else he didn't need, and I was ashamed of my constant insatiable hunger, for food and all manner of other things, everything I craved and wanted, and I have often envied others for similar reasons. Those who don't need to eat, who don't care about food and would never think to spend time in a kitchen because there is no pleasure to be had there for them. How freeing, I thought. I was like a woman on a diet fantasizing about how everything would be fine if only she were thin. I thought that people for whom food had no meaning couldn't possibly have a care in the world.

~

Later, after I left him and the apartment with the dining room and moved into the one-room apartment I would inhabit with my daughter every other week, I took the big white table with me. I put it in the middle of that one room with all the chairs around it, close to the windows so it would catch the light. I would use it as a dining table and a desk, and one day as I sat there working, trying to finish a piece of writing that I didn't know how to wrap up, I came to think of rice pudding. That's how it was, among other things. As soon as something felt difficult, food came to mind, and it could be any food at all, anything that would be more surveyable and manageable than my current task, and that someone else, hopefully, would also enjoy.

The thought of rice pudding made me hungry. I could already taste and smell it, its softness, the slight give to each grain, and instead of finishing my writing, I left the table and went into the kitchen. Should I make it for us for dinner, just like the one Grandma used to make for me and Grandad? It probably wouldn't be too complicated, and it was a good time to do something special since it was the first dinner my daughter and I would have together after being apart for a week.

She probably wouldn't want to taste it at first, like me at her age, but once she did she would love it, like I had. So I thought, and I pictured the pudding in front of me, sitting on the table in its usual dish, and at once I could see everything else in Grandma and Grandad's dark dinette. The pennants and plates, the spinning wheel in the corner, the pullout sofa I slept on the first night before I got into bed with them and Grandad had to move out there instead. I saw it all and felt it all.

―

When I was a child, 'rice pudding' was my answer to the question of what my favourite food was, but it was probably an unfashionable dish even then. No one else we knew ate rice pudding, and over the years, I've never met anyone who liked it or even knew what it was.

My mother had probably seen my grandmother making rice pudding, but she was never around when we ate it and would barely taste the one Grandma left with us. I was about to try to recreate a dish and imagined I was the only one who knew how it should taste, and I thought it would be a way of telling my daughter about my grandmother and grandfather, and in doing so also say something about myself that perhaps she should know, something I didn't know how to communicate myself and wasn't even quite sure of what it was.

Our life together was so different to the one I'd had with them. She had never met them because they died before she was born, she had never been in a home that looked like theirs, never spent time with people like the ones they used to spend time with, nor eaten what they used to eat. But if she got a taste of rice pudding, surely she'd discover something about all that, I thought, something that was impossible to convey otherwise. She'd get a piece of it inside her, just like I had it inside of me.

—

For me, food meant so much. My physical hunger was one part, but the other ways in which I hungered, and the ever-present craving that seemed to reside within me, were greater. I'd gotten accustomed to turning to food for the fulfillment of all my needs, and the effects of eating had reached so deeply inside me that I lost all sense of the meaning behind it.

I took a seat at the big white table and told myself I should finish my work first, but after only a short while I started looking for recipes instead. A few months earlier I'd been on a business trip to Italy, a couple days of which were spent at a family-run farm in Tuscany, perched atop a hill with a dining room overlooking the valley and the fields. There was no menu at its small restaurant, rather the chef served whatever he felt like making with the ingredients at hand. On the first evening he'd taken me aside after the appetizer – grilled bread with oil, and fried artichokes, which I later learned to make myself – to inform me that there would be cake for dessert and through his inquiries he'd learned that I did not like cake. He said I could have an alternative, perhaps fruit or chocolate, but if I did taste the cake I would not regret it.

I felt like a child as he spoke to me. It was a familiar feeling and it made me feel close to him even though he was a stranger. Later, when I tasted the cake he'd baked, I understood why he'd been so insistent. I could identify with him, with what I perceived as his desire to persuade with his food and win over all skeptics. His cake was unlike any other I'd taken pains to sample in order to please people and which would make me retch. It had a light mouth feel, its sweetness fresh not sickly, and when he came out to make sure I'd tasted it, he laughed at my almost empty dessert plate and said *Brava,* and the next evening in the dining room I even found myself looking forward to having more of his cake, but when dessert arrived I saw that he'd made something else.

On the small plates the waitress was carrying out was something yellow and golden. I thought it looked like a Tosca cake, but when I forked a small bite and saw the pattern below the surface, I realized it was a rice pudding. I'd never imagined that such a thing might exist in Italy. It was sweeter than my grandmother's, with almond liqueur and a sprinkling of candied orange peel bits on top, and if Grandma's reminded me of anything Italian, it was risotto. Hers was not a dessert but a main course, buttery and creamy, and unlike a Tuscan torta di riso, it was served hot.

—

The recipes I found on the web recommended serving rice pudding with saftsås, fruit juice thickened with corn starch, or lingonberry jam. None of them mentioned anything about serving it with an extra knob of butter like Grandma did, and not a single one had raisins on the ingredient list, but in the comment section I saw that a woman had noted that there should be raisins. I read a few more descriptions and realized that rice pudding was usually prepared as a dessert here in Sweden too, 'rice pudding cake,' as it was referred to somewhere, but I wasn't going to make that kind.

I went down to the shop and bought a carton of unpasteurized milk and a packet of porridge rice, the kind you use at Christmas to make porridge and the rice à la Malta that Grandma used to make with canned tangerine wedges, and as soon as I was back in my apartment I got to it, even though I'd intended to do my work. I put my hair up, washed my hands, and took out Grandma's old apron, held it in my hands, and found her scent in the fibres of the fabric.

—

As a child, I never needed that scent to evoke her, the weight of her body next to mine, and how it felt when she lifted her arms and wrapped them around me. Back then I knew exactly what to do to make it feel like she was sitting with me even when she wasn't. I could feel her embrace whenever I liked. I thought about her every day and prayed to God for her to go on living so I could keep her. I was so afraid that she would die and be lost to me and I knew this was a possibility because she was so old. Grandad was old too and they'd both told me that God didn't exist; nonetheless I asked God to give me a little more time with them. In spite of this and in spite of everything else they said, I prayed for them to be in this life a little longer.

What would I do if my mother and my grandmother vanished? I thought about it often and I supposed that I shouldn't really be praying to God because I didn't belong to him. I knew this to be true and I knew that he knew, because he saw and sensed everything I did. It was complicated. I belonged to another, and yet I was the only one of us who believed in him and the only one who understood that he could always see us and everything we did.

He saw me each time I did something I wasn't allowed, like when I snuck food from Grandma or Mom and ate it up and then pretended I had no idea where it had gone. He knew I lied and stole food and treats when I craved them and so he knew how dishonest and weak I was. He knew about all the times I'd pilfered such things and all the times I wanted to be alone and eat and not have to deal with everyone else. He knew all about my selfishness and could see into my thoughts as I was thinking them, and this is why I had to think right, and I really did try, but even when I did, bad thoughts still lurked behind the good ones, and to him they were in full view.

—

Even so, I prayed every day and every night for his help, even though I was who I was and even though nothing in his universe was made for me. I didn't fit into the world over which he ruled and I didn't fit into my mother's and grandmother's worlds either. I was always kind, like they were, and I was grateful, like they had taught me to be; still I could really lose my temper and they never did, they never failed to be kind, and it seemed like they couldn't get angry, not at me anyway. Grandma got angry when a rich relative we didn't know spoke out on television about how taxes should be lowered, and Mom got angry at my teachers when they said things to me that she didn't agree with, like how we weren't a family because it was just her and me. But they were otherwise so gentle and mild, and it was strange: anger could overwhelm me at any moment and make me want to claw my way out of myself.

Mom would let me sink my teeth into her hands when that happened, and drag my nails along her forearms. I would claw deep white marks or grab her skin with my hands and twist. I grabbed a pencil and jammed it in my cheek so hard it left a grey mark next to my mouth – there's still a small dot there. I tore up my drawings and destroyed photos of myself. I wanted to fight and break things, like people in television shows or like Grandma that one time I've never told anyone in our family about – when she was in the kitchen washing the dishes after dinner as usual and suddenly let out a soft scream and pushed all the plates into the sink, shattering every one.

Looking back on this memory now, I find it just as difficult to comprehend, but I'm absolutely sure this did happen. I'd leapt up from my seat at the kitchen table where I'd been drawing, my pencils scattered over the oilcloth as usual, but once I was at her side, looking up at her face, she peered down at me as if nothing had happened. She looked like she usually did when she gazed at me, as if she were about to crack a smile and hum a tune or break into song. Her face was as soft and open as ever, and she was perfectly calm as she gathered the shards into her hands and opened the door to the garbage cabinet and threw them away.

I thought about it many times afterwards, how that little scream she emitted sounded like something that needed to come out of her, and once when my daughter was little and I felt so stuck in that big apartment with a dining room, I'd done the same thing. I enjoyed the feeling of crossing a line, taking the plate in my hand and hearing the wet porcelain break against the sink and the tile behind it, and I wondered if Grandma had felt the same strange joy inside her when she did it.

I put on her apron and knotted the long ties around my waist, took out a saucepan, measured the rice and rinsed it, poured in three-quarters of the creamy milk, and lit the gas flame on the stove. Then I bent down and opened the oven door and turned on the gas while pressing the igniter until long rows of small blue flames rose up inside the oven. On the bottom were some charred bits that must have been left over from a batch of bread, and I could see that the interior was thick with soot.

I often turned to baking when I couldn't get anything else done or when a void flared inside me and I needed to try to fill it. Since the large white table did not fit in the eating area in the kitchen, I'd put a small couch there so my daughter could curl up and watch children's programs on a small television, or draw, or do other things while I baked or cooked or washed the dishes and cleaned the kitchen. I imagined that I'd be doing those things in there with a brand-new lightness and joy, when it was just her and me, and so it was. I mixed sourdough starters in glass jars and put them on the spice rack above the stove and bought unsulfured organic apricots from which I captured wild yeast that was placed on top of the fridge where it was warm; I made croissants, pasta, and baguettes, and in the beginning I was so surprised that I managed it all without much issue, that I could actually make most of it taste good and look like it should.

Most of all I enjoyed the time-consuming things that had many steps. Feeling the bread dough against my fingers, its transformation as I kneaded and stretched it, watching it change with time and temperature as it rose. Baking itself was not easy with the gas oven. It looked like the tin dollhouse stove that my mother had as a child and that my grandmother had given me the time my grandfather and mother built me a dollhouse on the bookshelf in my room. The knobs were fiddly and there was only a small glass pane on the oven door through which to look. Actually, I might have liked that most of all: sitting on the floor in front of the oven and watching something bake, its rising and the soft surface hardening and changing colour, just like the recipe predicted. It brought me a kind of comfort that something could be this simple and overseeable, so distinct from everything else, perceptible and possible to control. The knowledge that everything would turn out as it should, if only you read up on what wasn't immediately clear to you and were meticulous enough in your actions.

It was logical, unlike so much else. I turned the gas to the second-highest mark. The rice pudding needed forty-five minutes in the oven at two hundred degrees, but it was impossible to set a precise temperature, and I hadn't put a thermometer inside the oven because I hadn't yet realized I needed to. I simply had to hope for the best while keeping an eye on the rice pudding. It should be firm and have a nice surface but feel creamy inside. Under no circumstances should it dry out. If it did, the shopping and all my work would be in vain.

—

From what my mother had told me about her childhood, I'd understood that it had been different then, but when I was little, Grandma was always at home. In her kitchen she usually wore the plaid apron over her house-coat. She wasn't very tall or big, but her body still looked substantial – the way her flesh bulged seemed to be an invitation to touch it.

The skin on her lower legs had small webs of blue veins that were almost fully concealed by her brown stockings, and her fingers were usually swollen and thick like the fresh sausages Grandad would bring home when he took the ferry to do the shopping. She'd hold her hands up in front of her, scrutinizing and squeezing. Well, I'll be, she would say, and pinch the bottom of one finger so the skin tightened around what was underneath. I wasn't sure I could see it, but she said the lymphatic fluid wasn't moving around her body as it should and was accumulating in certain places. But a person shouldn't complain, she said. Not at my age.

My own fingers were also swollen and my hands were often a little red or almost purple just like hers could be. She painted her nails with a pink varnish that seemed to chip right away, and I sometimes wondered why she insisted on wearing it. She never protected her hands when she was doing something, never put on gloves while cleaning unless she was clearing drains or polishing the old copper pots that hung on the wall.

As a rule, the apron was the only thing she'd use as protection. The plaid fabric strained across her belly and breasts, and I sometimes wondered how she who ate so little could be so large. She often refused food, maybe helping herself to just a potato and a slice of bread with some butter. I know when she was younger it was important that women eat in moderation, which is probably still true today; the precept that women not eat with wild abandon is perhaps the very reason why some of us do. Or one of the reasons.

But I never once remember thinking that she might be trying to fulfill an image of femininity through her approach to eating. Something about the way I perceived her made me think she didn't do that kind of thing. She seemed so artless compared to other women I saw, and it never struck me that she might also want to be slim and elegant and not take up so much space, that maybe she thought this was the way we should be.

—

She'd nibble while working in the kitchen or doing something else, and perhaps that was why she was never really hungry at actual meals. The food you ate in the evening at Grandma and Grandad's was called kvällsmat, supper, usually sandwiches or a few small plates with leftovers: a bunch of radishes or a small bowl of salad with chives. Grandad drank tea or a small bottle of dark beer and I drank milk. They'd buy skimmed milk for me ahead of my visits, and later, when a variant came along that was even more skimmed than the previous skimmed milk, they'd buy that one.

Kvällsmat could be eaten in front of the television while watching the news or at the small table in the kitchen. Their kitchen was long and narrow and not big, just like ours. There was no fan above the stove, only a round vent you opened by pulling a chain before you fried something. A haze of grease would quickly spread throughout the apartment. Above the stove was also a roll of paper coated in a thin layer of grease and a pencil stub dangling from a string. She wrote down everything that needed buying on that paper. The cupboards above the sink were at an angle and had space-saving sliding doors, but there was an eating area big enough for the small table with the oilcloth. On top of the oilcloth was another cloth, a small doily on which the transistor radio was placed and often the bread basket, usually with the pale rye crisp bread we'd brought for Grandad, covered with a napkin. On the windowsill were some cut milk cartons with seeds in them and at one side of the table was the door to the kitchen balcony, where they grew chives and radishes and marigolds in flower boxes and stored some of the food, and bottles of light beer and Sockerdricka, an old-fashioned soft drink, in a crate.

Dinner was a meal served in the dinette in the middle of the day. It was a dinette and not a dining room. And one day they managed to get me to taste the rice pudding. I don't know how it happened, what they did or said, or if they'd simply finally succeeded in wearing me down after all their many attempts. They liked rice pudding so much that my grandmother made it probably once a week, so there had been many occasions. I don't remember if it was something about how it looked or smelled that made me change my mind, but I don't think so. I think it was just how it goes: that day was different somehow. She put a small piece on my plate as usual, and after I decided the time had come, I hesitantly brought the fork to my mouth. She looked at me with surprise and her face lit up as I chewed and swallowed; she and Grandad studied me closely as I took another bite and then another and finally turned my full attention to the plate in front of me and ate it all up.

When I asked for more they laughed, and there was a palpable calm in the small room. It was as if they were exhaling, I thought. The taste was nothing like I'd imagined it. The browned surface was chewy and salty and the rice smooth, with regular bursts of warm sweetness from the raisins. It was the best thing I'd ever eaten in my life. They laughed again when I said that, because my life hadn't been very long, especially not compared to theirs, but in that moment I wasn't making comparisons. I was simply so happy and surprised that this was possible: something I'd always thought was bad could turn out to be very, very good.

—

As for them, rice pudding wasn't something they'd eaten as children. Back then, everything was tight, as Grandma said. She wrote those words to me once, in her scrolling hand that was sometimes hard for me to decipher. I'd sent her a letter with a series of questions for a school assignment, along with a few college-ruled pages from a notebook, which she wrote her answers on, then mailed back. We usually ate cabbage dishes, she wrote. She could smell the cabbage cooking at a distance when she was on her way home from school and wouldn't want to go inside because she was so tired of eating it. She did not use words such as *hunger* or *necessity*. She wrote that her father would sometimes borrow a horse and cart and go off to try to buy eggs and milk and butter from the farmers, and when he succeeded, it was call for celebration upon his return.

These were the kinds of ingredients they'd have needed to make a rice pudding. Of course, rice and raisins weren't things they had either. I compared a few recipes online and came up with my own interpretation, which I wrote down, and brought the piece of paper with me into the kitchen and placed it on the counter in front of me. The heat from the gas oven and from the stove made me sweat, and the white paper became stained with milk and butter and water. I hadn't really been able to foresee how long it would take me to make this one – and really very simple – dish. It was not at all complicated, but I didn't have an intuitive understanding of how to make it. It had never before occurred to me to cook a dish my grandmother had served, I mostly made noodles with vegetables and fish or marinated tofu when I was cooking for only myself and my daughter; husmanskost, hearty home cooking, was new to me. At each step, I had to check the recipe to make sure I'd understood.

While the rice and milk simmered on the gas flame and the smell slowly spread in the small apartment, I fit in some work. When the porridge was ready, it needed to be left to cool so it would thicken. I cracked three large eggs into a bowl and whisked them with half a decilitre of cold milk from the fridge. I added the gleaming grainy mass plus a handful of raisins and stirred the mixture with a wooden spoon until everything was combined. Then I greased the pan, poured the batter in, and put it in the oven, and while the rice pudding was baking, I finished the writing I needed to do, pausing a few times, only briefly, to go into the kitchen, bend down, and peer through the sooty window. When the egg timer went off, I shut the computer and opened the oven door.

—

I could feel myself being drawn to food precisely because it was quotidian and straightforward and served an unassailable function. I was used to being hesitant and doubting myself, my own thoughts, and everything I did, but cooking was something that had to be done and it imparted a sense of calm; I felt I was being put to good use when I cooked and that everything fell into place even when what I was cooking stressed me out or was too challenging.

I slipped on the oven mitts my mother had given me and took the pan out of the oven. The rice pudding was ready and my eyes couldn't see their fill of it. It looked perfect. I set it down on the sink and hurried off to pick up my daughter. She'd been allowed to stay at her old preschool even after I moved out of the district, and to get there I had to ride the metro, change to another line, then catch a bus. The round trip took more than an hour and a half, and most days I dreaded the journey.

At the same time I missed her and I held such a strong image in my mind of what it would be like to see her again. She'd come running toward me and throw herself around my neck and I would hug her. We'd buy flowers on the way home, as I imagined mothers did on Fridays, I'd let her hold them in her seat on the carriage, and when we got home I'd serve her the rice pudding I'd made and tell her about my mother's own parents and what it was like when I was a child.

But when I arrived at the preschool, I immediately noticed how the week had tired her out and I could feel how tired I was myself. The simple act of gathering her things and coaxing her out the door was an effort, but it took everything in me not to think about the fact that all I wanted to do was lie down. Once we were on the bus, I asked her what they had for lunch, which was always my first question when she was little, as if there was nothing else that interested me, and then I told her about the rice pudding, how it had become my favourite dish when I was little after I finally agreed to have a bite of it and that I'd made one for us for dinner so she could try it too.

She nodded along as I talked, and while we were still on the bus everything was fine, but she whined the rest of the way home. She was probably a bit too big for the stroller, but our trips to and from the preschool tuckered her out so much that I'd started taking the stroller with me to make it there on time. I no longer cared what people thought or that old ladies might approach us with concern to ask if she hadn't outgrown her stroller. Often she walked by herself, but as we were coming out of the metro, she refused. I had to push the stroller up the steep ramp that ran alongside the stairs, and when we'd emerged she asked for a hamburger and started bawling when I said no.

Her request hadn't come out of the blue – we'd often eaten at that McDonald's. It was never planned, it just happened, sometimes several times a week and often even if I didn't think we would. It wasn't more expensive than shopping and then doing your own cooking, quite the opposite. We used to sit by the window and eat our fish burgers and look out over the square and the intersection, and the restaurant would be packed with people, a lot of lone parents with children who were crying and screaming or had fallen asleep in their strollers and a lot of other people who couldn't make dinner, who were on their way to or from their jobs and didn't have the energy or the time to cook even for themselves.

But that night the rice pudding was waiting for us. When we entered the apartment, I was so exhausted and so hungry that I was shaking. I went straight into the kitchen. I'd thought I'd have to reheat it in the oven, but when I put my hand on the outside of the pan, it was still hot. I set out plates and cutlery, lit the candles in the candlesticks, and placed the rice pudding on the big white table. It looked exactly as it should, exactly like my grandmother's, and I was so happy I'd managed to make it.

—

My grandmother must have been driven by the image of who she was supposed to be, a postwar wife and mother. But I too had a variety of images of who I wanted to be. I was so full of desires and expectations for my life that I didn't seem able to realize without abandoning myself. When I took the rice pudding out of the oven that afternoon, I'd imagined how the evening would proceed down to the last detail, and as I turned off the gas and hung up my apron, I pictured our dinner with the rice pudding. How we would sit down and eat together and how I would show her who I was and all the love I had, for her and for those who came before us and were no longer alive.

The rice pudding would tell her everything I couldn't about them and about where I came from, everything she never asked about but still needed to know somehow. But when I put the pan on the big white table and asked her to come sit down, she didn't want to. Not now, she said. She was lying on the couch in the kitchen, fiddling with something. Sure, but do come now before it gets cold, I said. I want you to taste it and it's not as good when it's cold.

I looked at the rice pudding in its pan and could hardly believe I'd made it myself. It looked exactly like Grandma's, like what I'd so often seen her place on the table. I repeated my request until she finally strolled over to the table and sat down on her chair, and I felt myself exhale. I was so tired and hungry, as I always was after I'd gone to and from the preschool to pick her up in the late afternoon. I couldn't wait to sit down and eat and talk to her, but once we were in our chairs I could barely get a word out. Fatigue left me at a loss, and I wasn't even sure of what I'd wanted to say in the first place.

—

I told her again that this was the rice pudding my grandmother used to make for me. The baked surface was like a thin skin over the smooth interior and it split when I drove the knife in. I cut a piece, which I put on her plate, and ate one myself. I took a small forkful and brought it to my mouth. My daughter was watching as I started to eat, and I felt the warmth of the rice pudding spread through me.

It was just hot enough and had the desired creamy texture, and yet something wasn't right. I took another bite. It didn't taste like I remembered. I thought there must be something missing, but the recipe contained only a few ingredients, and I, not usually one to follow recipes, had followed it to the letter.

Sure, it could have used more salt – I hadn't yet learned to salt my food properly then, we never had real salt at home when I was little because it was considered unhealthy at the time – and I probably hadn't used enough butter either, not as much as Grandma would have anyway. But there was something else too. I was a different person and my taste buds had changed, and if I was no longer the same person, then rice pudding wouldn't taste the same either. It was obvious, really. It just hadn't occurred to me.

—

The flavour was bland compared to everything else I ate, and it wasn't as good as I thought it would be. And yet the rice pudding quickly disappeared into me. I ate cautiously at first to focus on the taste, but then I wanted to devour the whole plate in front of me, not because it tasted amazing but simply because I wanted to swallow it down in one. That happened sometimes. When eating with others, I'd take my time, but when I was alone, something might come over me and I'd want to consume everything all at once.

I tried to stop myself but couldn't. It was as if I were getting hungrier with each bite. I finished my first portion, then cut another piece from the pan before my daughter had even started on hers; it lay before her untouched as she sat there twirling her waterglass and talking about… I don't know. I can't really remember what we used to talk about when we'd sit there together for breakfast or lunch or dinner, or even what it was like to dine alone with such a small child. But I always wanted us to sit down and eat together each in our own chair at the big white table.

Absent-mindedly, she plunged her fork into the rice pudding, prodding the rice grains and the butter and the hot rehydrated raisins, but instead of putting what she found in her mouth and tasting it, she put her fork back down and spread the pudding around on the plate. I watched her play with her food. All you have to do is taste it, I said. Just a little. Then she dug her fork back in, fished out another bite, and held it up, examining it with an indifferent, almost disgusted, expression.

—

I was so sure my daughter would love rice pudding. I'd envisioned how I would end up making it for her again and again after that first time and how wonderful it would be to be a mother standing at the stove making her child's favourite food and remembering how she'd eaten the same thing when she was little. But her experience of the rice pudding differed from mine. The moral I'd drawn from my story was that agreeing to try something new might reward you with a new favourite dish – and what a reward it was for me – but to her, my story meant nothing, and in fact her reaction largely supported what I'd heard from dietitians and others, that children may need to be exposed to a new dish up to forty-two times before they decide to try it.

—

I suppose that's what had happened with me at Grandma and Grandad's when I was her age. The rice pudding had been on my plate so many times; each time Grandma had asked me to taste just a little and finally she must have worn me down. This was my daughter's first exposure, but I had none of Grandma's patience. I couldn't imagine making rice pudding forty more times in hopes she'd change her mind. All I wanted was for her to take a bite right now and see how good it was. Surely it would taste better to her, I thought.

But she wouldn't eat.

I helped myself to a little more, dumbstruck. As I ate in silence, everything I thought I could convey with the dinner I'd prepared, the whole story of who we really were, slipped into a void before my eyes. When I looked down at the rice pudding again, it appeared so meaningless. Why had I gotten it into my head that I should make this and then make such a big deal of it? Why did I spend the afternoon on this instead of my work, and why did I insist on carrying out little projects such as these in a bid to stage my vision of how our family should be, aided by shared activity around that table? It didn't have to be food – other things could bring us to the table as well, such as sewing or drawing, in exactly the way I envisioned. But very often it was food.

Neither of us said a word.

I felt empty and kept eating in order to fill the emptiness. I ate and ate, but the emptiness kept spreading as I was finishing my plate and the silence rested between us. I couldn't say any of what I'd wanted to say or show any of what I'd wanted to show, because I couldn't get anything out. My mouth was full. I sat there in silence, eating and feeling disappointed in myself.

When I'd polished off the whole plate, I made one last attempt. I begged. Please taste it, I said. Just a little. It's really good. She picked up her fork, then put it back down on her plate and looked at me. I've tasted it, she said. It was good. I'm full. And with that she jumped down from her chair and left without having taken the tiniest bite of what I'd prepared for her, which was less a dish and more a material representation of the basis of my entire existence.

I got up from my chair and said she hadn't tasted even a little bit, and she said, Yes I have and now I want ice cream.

In my memory it's both lit by a bright flash and foggy. I remember trying not to get angry. I did this all day long, it was probably what I'd always done. I'd try to contain my anger and suppress it so it wouldn't come out, and now I was trying to stop it from reaching her.

Have you tasted it? I asked in a voice that already bore traces of something hard and unpleasant, it didn't sound quite like my own, and when she again said yes, I noticed that I was no longer breathing. It felt like I wasn't getting any air. I paced alongside the big white table. I told her she hadn't even tasted it, and when she yet again claimed that she had, I opened my mouth and heard myself shout the question one more time.

It was like breaking a barrier. Have you tasted it? I shouted. Have you? She was standing completely still, and I thought she looked even smaller than she was, as if she were shrinking before my eyes. It would have felt so good to just give up and let the anger take over, but as I stood there in the middle of the room yelling at her, I thought about what an idiot I was, behaving like this toward a child.

—

It was as if nothing existed anymore, nothing inside her and nothing inside me. There was only the air between us, filled by my barking and my gestures. I could have tolerated her rejecting my offering, but not her lying about it and wanting lots of other things. I too wanted so much that I couldn't have, and how should a parent relate to a child's every desire or even the fact that she and I were two separate people? Most of all, I couldn't tolerate myself, my own anger, and how my powerlessness in the face of this paralyzed me.

I screamed at her one more time before suddenly coming to my senses and stopping myself. She'd sunk to the floor in front of the table, I sat down next to her and apologized and she apologized and then I lay on the floor next to her and felt ashamed of myself. I couldn't turn around and put my arms around her and pull her close like I wanted to and like I knew I should. All I could feel was her little hand on my back, the floor beneath me like a vortex, and my own judgment of myself. In that moment all I wanted was to disappear, and that's how I experienced it; it was as if I left my body and drifted away from it, rising higher and higher until I was floating above us like a great open eye taking in and registering everything.

I saw myself there so clearly on the floor and her, her little body next to mine and her hand on me. Next to us I saw the big white table set for dinner, the candlelight still flickering and the flames reflected in the windows, her plate with the cutlery beside it and the untouched food and my own with only a few glossy grains of rice left.

Everything seemed so unbearably clear to me and I had only one thought in my head: I was a child myself. How could I not have seen it? I'd always been told how mature I was, practically an adult even though I was only a child, but now that I actually was an adult, and in terms of days and years had undoubtedly left childhood behind, I could see this was false. I hadn't grown up. Her hand kept moving across my back; of the two of us, she was the adult, I thought, and the thought was almost impossible to bear.

As I remember it, I spent summers and Christmas holidays with Grandma and Grandad, and whenever else my mother needed time to herself to do something or travel somewhere. The first time she left me with them, I didn't understand what was happening. I was little then, maybe I shouldn't be able to remember it and maybe it's not a memory but something that arose in another way – that image of the rooms in their apartment and me walking around in them after she left.

From the living room, I walked through the hallway to the dinette and through the kitchen and out into the hallway again, crying and moving back and forth across the brown wall-to-wall carpet, trying to get rid of the sting and ache inside me, and I remember Grandma picking me up. She put me on her lap and comforted and held me. Did she give me something to eat then too? Did she get up and carry me off to the candy bowl on the low dark cupboard by the wall, or did I walk over and help myself?

I couldn't reach it yet and I don't know what kind of candy was in there, maybe Polkagris candy canes, which Grandad liked, or milk-chocolate-covered puffed rice and those little white-and-jade-green salty licorice sticks that were part of the bridge mix Grandma used to buy. But every time I was given a piece of candy and ate it up, a warm calm spread through me and then I'd be alert to the presence of the bowl. It would become like a magnet, a centre point in Grandma and Grandad's apartment around which all my movements revolved.

—

Later, I'd sleep with my grandmother in the double bed in the bedroom because I couldn't fall asleep alone, but on the very first night I spent at their apartment I lay awake on the kitchen sofa bed in the dinette thinking about how time was stretching out before me like a long grey ribbon. I couldn't tell when she would finally return, if she'd return at all. It was uncertain. Lots of things could happen to a person, I'd understood. I looked at the darkness beyond the window and it frightened me that she was somewhere out there and I could do nothing to make her come back.

The dinette was unrecognizable at night. To avoid seeing the darkness around me, I tried to keep my eyes shut as I lay there. It felt like I'd never be able to fall asleep, but I must have managed somehow, and when morning came, everything was different. The room was aglow with the slender rays of sunlight that had found their way through the window under the drawn blinds, and I felt strangely full of anticipation for no reason at all. From the kitchen came the faint sound of radio chatter and the clinking of Grandad's teacup as he set it down on its saucer, but I realized it was the smell that had woken me up. An aroma had wafted across the room to where I lay.

I climbed off the pullout couch and saw Grandad at the kitchen table. In his large hands were two slices of bread that he'd taken out of the toaster next to him on the table and that I'd barely noticed before. He put one in the bread basket and the other on a small plate in front of him. I could hear the crunch and scratch as he spread it with butter, and the closer I came, the better I could smell it: the bread, the marmalade in the jar, the lid of which he'd just unscrewed, and the steam from the tea. Apricot and bergamot.

I'd never smelled toast before, we didn't have a toaster, I'd never seen bagged sandwich bread, and when my grandmother lifted me onto the chair opposite my grandfather and took one of the slices of bread and put it on a plate she set down in front of me, it was like being enveloped in softness. She fixed me a cup of chamomile tea, because children weren't supposed to drink black tea, and as I began to eat, I noticed that the taste of toasted bread with melted butter flowed out and settled on top of everything else.

—

Grandma knew a lot about things, such as which teas children should and should not drink, that you shouldn't put honey in hot tea because it would lose its healing properties, she knew what eased the hiccups and what was good when you were sick or couldn't sleep, and she knew which weeds and leaves to place on wounds and which to pick and chew if you had a pain somewhere. She said there was a bounty growing right by their apartment building. I learned that my grandfather drank tea with milk at breakfast and black coffee later in the morning and that I'd get toast for breakfast when I was with them, because that's what he ate.

All those mornings I spent there, I'd sit opposite him with my slice of toast on the plate in front of me, trying to find ways to make the toast last longer. First, I'd watch it for a while: the shift from white to pale yellow and golden and brown, or even black if it had burned and Grandma had scraped off the char over the sink, still some sooty grains would remain, and how the surface would soften as the butter melted and dispersed in pale contiguous islands.

I'd eat the crust first, gnawing it off with my front teeth like a rabbit, and then I ate the rest of the bread with the smallest bites I could manage. I ate and noticed how it filled me, and one morning it occurred to me that I might be able to ask for a second slice.

I had no idea if this was possible, and it took a few days for me to decide; I was waiting for what seemed to be exactly the right moment. After I asked, Grandma stopped right in the middle of the rag rug on the floor. She looked at me. But my dear little heart, she said, casting herself forward to hug me. You can have as many as you like!

She gestured with her hands around the bread bag as if to demonstrate how big it was. Huge. There were so many slices, endless amounts of bread in the bag, plus an extra loaf in the freezer. If I felt the slightest bit hungry, I could eat. Nothing would ever run out at Grandma and Grandad's, and if it did, they could just go to the store in the shopping centre across the street and buy more.

Then she started laughing and Grandad laughed too and I wasn't quite sure what was funny, but I liked the way Grandma looked at me and held me, and her reassurance grew within me. I was allowed to take more, just like I was allowed to help myself to the candy bowl even though I almost didn't want to because I knew I wouldn't be able to stop thinking about it later, I'd want more even though I was so full I felt sick, and I learned where the bread bag was and that I was allowed to open it and help myself. During breakfast or at any other time.

I took two slices at once, twisted the bag shut and reattached the little piece of plastic like Grandma had shown me, and then I put the bread in the toaster and depressed the slider on one end until I heard a clack inside. Then I sat there feeling the heat build as I sensed the smell spread through the air, listened to the low electric hum, and tried to predict the exact moment when the slices would fly into the air.

—

I'm not sure if Grandma ate breakfast, I don't think I ever saw her do it. I never saw her sit down and eat in the morning. In the evenings she cut up slices of buttermilk loaf and Danish rye bread and made our sandwiches in the kitchen, and I suppose she'd take a bite of something during the process, but it was only at dinner that she sat down to eat. Otherwise she always cooked for us; I'd see her standing at the stove or moving between it and the kitchen counter and the refrigerator and the pantry or the cold storage on the kitchen balcony, and she seemed to be chewing near-constantly.

She'd become a pescatarian long before anyone used that word. She ate fish, and eggs and dairy products and cottage cheese and sprouts and raw carrots were staples in her refrigerator. She had her vitamins and medicine for goitre. On a shelf in the pantry were small bottles of tinctures and extracts of roots and herbs, which she dropped into water and drank to help her sleep better or to make her feel more alert and lighter on her feet on certain days when her goitre was acting up.

Apart from the fact that her thyroid wasn't working properly, which must have made her tired even though I never noticed it, she was never sick and Grandad and Mom were never sick either. They were never in pain and did not complain about anything, physical or otherwise. They were never sad or worried. I did not understand why I'd ended up with itchy skin, a head that tended to ache, and a body with unpredictable pains and nausea and unpleasant sensations. I always thought I'd grow up to be as imperturbable as they were. I made a point of remembering everything my grandmother told me about vitamins and valerian and plantain herb, marigold and meadowsweet. As she saw it, what you ate and drank kept you healthy and strong. She sprouted her own peas and seeds, had a plastic raw juice extractor into which she put leftover fruits and vegetables to make cold-pressed juices, and she never drank anything with her food because, according to her, it was bad for digestion.

Where did she get it all from? I wonder if the magazines she sometimes sat with, in which I thought she was reading cake recipes and gardening tips and accounts of compelling life stories, also contained articles on how women should take care of themselves, what to eat and what not to eat and how much or little.

—

She never ate much when it was time for a sit-down meal, but otherwise chances were she had something in her mouth. It always looked like she'd just popped something in, but not so much that she couldn't still walk around and chat with me as she would or sing the songs she'd sing. While cooking and cleaning the kitchen, her jaws were constantly grinding, moving quickly as if duty-bound, as if she were a garbage disposal that had to process and swallow everything. A leftover piece of bread, half a radish, some soft butter that had escaped the package. She'd catch something on her finger and lick it off and then it was gone; she'd pick crumbs off the oilcloth-covered table and eat them or take something from the plates she'd just carried out.

She'd instruct me to finish what was on my plate, but even when I liked the food, I couldn't eat everything she dished up for me, and what

I left would be saved or eaten by her in passing, and the refrigerator shelves were full of leftovers waiting to be taken care of by her or taken out and thrown away when they started to spoil and rot.

I tried not to look at all the little containers and bowls and what was in there, nor at the stinky cheeses that Grandad shopped for on his ferry trips, during which he also bought himself liquor that he would sip occasionally and on holidays. While she was filling the fridge, she'd graze on leftovers or nibble on something she'd picked up in another room, from the candy or fruit bowl or from her handbag. The bag was made of imitation leather and suede in various shades of white, from the chalkiest of whites like our table to dark bone, and it could contain cough drops or a box of pastilles or a small package of biscuits. Or all of those things. If it was summer, it would contain a bag of peaches she'd bought at the market while waiting for the bus to their cottage in the community garden village.

—

Grandad didn't take the bus to the community garden, he'd cycle, which I assume she'd have done too had I not been with her. She had her own bicycle, but they didn't own a car and couldn't drive. Grandad would have two big panniers packed with beer and potatoes flanking the rear wheel of the bike. Once he tried to sit me on the rack as well, but I didn't have the strength to keep my legs elevated and one of my feet got caught in the spokes, so he had to make a sudden stop in the middle of the bike lane and almost caused a collision with another cyclist. Grandad managed to straighten the bike and climb off and pick me up and take my foot in his hands and blow away the pain so we could continue, but after that I'd ride the bus with Grandma.

She liked to chat awhile with the market vendors before selecting the loveliest peaches, and when we were on the bus she'd share them with me. I liked this, I liked the way each peach was split so it looked like a bottom, cleft with two round cheeks, like in my mother's paintings at home, but most of all I liked to watch my grandmother eat. It was so exciting and felt illicit somehow to watch her pink lips part and shut over and over again around the plump blushing fruit, and its fuzzy skin split and the peach juice dribbled down her fingers and her face took on that absent mien.

It looked as if she were being whisked away to a far-flung isolated place where no one could reach her, not even me who otherwise always could. It was unusual for her to absent herself, she who was otherwise always available, to me and to everyone else, every single person in our surroundings. She usually seemed so inviting and friendly, giving her full attention to the person in front of her, whoever it was, and waiting for whatever they had to say. It seemed as if she were in service, ever prepared for her environment, and I thought that was the way to be.

But with a peach in her hand, everything changed. None of that willingness to serve was apparent as she ate, she was interested only in the fruit and herself, turned inward toward the sensations. When she'd finished, she turned away and licked her fingers and wiped them with a cotton handkerchief in which she'd wrap the peach pit and put it in her handbag.

I found a special way of eating peaches too. I started by pressing my front teeth into the skin and biting a small flap and tearing at it to expose the flesh, glossy and wet. As I tore off a few more strips, the opening in the skin would take on a form that would announce itself if you spent time looking at it. A butterfly, a ship, a diamond. After that I took a bite of the exposed yellow flesh, as small as I could, and then another. I chewed, looked at the imprint of my teeth and felt the sweet, insipid peach flavour spread through my mouth. When the flesh was gone, I'd take my time with the pit. I wanted it to be completely exposed, the woody surface stripped of the fruit's fibres so that I could see all of the little wavy cracks and holes and the patterns they made. I'd use my front teeth to bite down on the tiny strands of pulp and pull them out.

—

I wanted everything I liked to last a long time, I loved the occupation that eating implied. When I was holding a peach, just like my grandmother, I was fully occupied. It was as if everything else was put on hold. I didn't need to think or talk, I didn't have to be afraid or long for my mother, I didn't have to do anything else or go anywhere. And nor were you supposed to do anything else while eating. You were supposed to concentrate on doing just that, right?

When I was with Grandma and Grandad and when they were with us, there'd be good food around and I remember thinking how strange it was that it worked each time. That something could be so reliable. Eating conjured sensations I could indulge in fully, it filled me physically and in all other respects; it was almost shocking that something so mundane and ordinary could have that power. I ate, and an excitement arose that made me feel both so alive and safe and like any other person on this earth. Or however I imagined they felt.

Back then, I don't really know if I understood that I was simultaneously being drawn away from them. I don't remember if I could feel it while it was happening or if it only became a fact with time. The food turned my interior into a hiding place to which I could retreat and remain undisturbed.

—

My mother had said that my grandmother liked peaches so much because that kind of fruit wasn't around when she was little. She loved bananas and watermelon and grapes too; where she grew up, there were only grey pears and apples, rock berries in the woods, and wild raspberries in thickets along the roads, wild strawberries that they threaded onto straws of grass and ate on the way home from school. She was used to foraging like that and she knew exactly what was edible and what was not.

In the only photo that exists of her whole family gathered together, she is sitting with two of her sisters on a kitchen sofa, perhaps the very one that was in their dinette and that I slept on that first night. She was the oldest of four daughters. When the picture was taken, the fourth was in her mother's belly. I would guess that Grandma is eight years old in that picture and the year is 1917; she has long braids, her father is wearing a hat to hide his bald spot, and in front of them on the table are books they've placed there for the benefit of the photographer, to indicate that they were readers, that they could read and their children would also learn how.

The photo is over a hundred years old and used to be in a steel frame on top of the linen cabinet in Grandma and Grandad's bedroom, a cabinet that held many bolts of fabric, porcelain fish on which to rest your butter knife at the dinner table, small forks with handles shaped like melon slices, and a teak jar in which they'd kept pastel-coloured cigarettes to offer to guests. Those were the days when people didn't know that smoking was dangerous, my mother would say when the subject came up. After it became public knowledge, they all stopped smoking.

The photo of Grandma with her parents and siblings had been placed near their wedding photo and other framed pictures of family members. I hated to see the photos they had of me because I didn't look at all like I felt – I looked bright and happy, but I felt the opposite. At home I scratched my own face out of all the photos, but in Grandma's home I didn't dare.

She had photo albums too, and the first time she took one out to show me, she flipped straight to a few pages of photos from the island my mom and I would visit, and pointed to a dark little photo of a man standing on a rock at sunset.

There's your dad, she said.

I thought he looked fantastic. He was standing so close to the sea in the glow of the sunset out there, right by the shell beach where I used to play in an old playpen they placed at the water's edge and where my mother had spent one late summer filling several small mini perfume bottles with the tiny shells she found in the sand. It was also strange, him having been there.

Later I saw pictures of my mother and father together, there on the island and elsewhere. In the little house on the hill above the plot that had belonged to my paternal grandfather, on beaches and rocks and boats and parties. There was something about the places they were in and the way everything around them looked that made them seem important and their lives lovely. I was convinced that my father must be an important person. What he was doing had to be important since he was living in a big city in another country, and not with us. He would write to me from different countries and places, and I would fantasize about who he was and everything he was doing.

I didn't hear my father spoken of very often, but when I did, I wanted to soak it all up, every word that communicated something about him. I didn't know much about my mother's life with him and I didn't dare ask, but I thought about it all the time. What little she did say was mostly about food. What they'd eaten and what he liked, which restaurants they'd been to, what he cooked when guests visited from overseas. The dinners they had around the big white table and how she was taught things like how to grill scallops and mix ice-cold dry martinis for them to sip before the meal.

I was so surprised when I realized my mom and dad had been together for a long time before she left him. I'd never imagined that either of them had intended for me, a child, to come into being. I'd had that thought often and it made me feel kind of bashful in the face of life as a whole, like someone who'd crashed a party. But when I did dare ask her, she said it wasn't true. It had been a planned pregnancy, and leading up to it they'd had a long relationship, one that had been going on for many years. We'd been longing for you, she said.

I didn't believe it.

Sometimes I thought about what it would be like when I grew up and maybe I could go visit him where he lived. He used to send me postcards and sometimes when the phone rang in my mother's bedroom he'd be on the other end of the line. She told me to talk to him, but I was afraid to. It was tough. I was afraid to talk and didn't know what to say. His voice was light and dry, like the gravel on the sidewalk outside our house in spring, and it had a faraway sound, as if he were calling to me from a distance.

⁓

Before he visited our home for the first time, as far as I knew and could remember, I had only ever seen him in that photograph from the island. It was an ordinary weekday evening. I don't remember what I'd eaten for dinner or if we were supposed to have eaten together, but I do remember that my mother had bought a small bottle of soda water that she never otherwise had at home, because that's what he drank.

Actually, his beverage was probably mineral water, but it might not have been available in our grocery store. After I'd eaten, we waited a long time for him. It was late, it was dark outside, and it felt like hours had passed by the time the doorbell finally rang and my mother went into the hall to answer it. I didn't dare go look. I could hardly believe he was in our apartment, on our street that was so far from where he lived and all the other places from which he used to write me. It seemed impossible, but there they were, standing in the hallway talking. Mom called to me but I ran into the living room and jumped onto the couch. She led him in and he sat down in the armchair, our regular old armchair in front of the window. When I looked in that direction, I thought there must be some mistake. This wasn't my father. This wasn't what he looked like. This man looked pale, his hair was almost blond or grey, and his face was also pale and maybe even a bit pinkish like mine, and he seemed so quiet and withdrawn.

I hadn't imagined him like this.

I don't remember if he said anything, but I remember being silent. I couldn't get a word out. This can't be him, I thought. He was wearing a suit, just like a dad on our street who Mom had said was a maître d', which I understood was something important because of how he'd dress. My mother went to get the soda water and I wanted her to come back right away, but she took a long time. He smiled at me and said something, but I couldn't answer. When she reappeared in the living room, she gave him the clear sparkling drink in a glass from which I drank milk. Maybe it was him, after all, I thought, only I didn't recognize him, but it was still wrong to see him in our ordinary space holding my glass.

Mom had her usual mug of tea and sat down with it next to me on the sofa. I'd spent the whole day in preschool and had been looking forward to this evening, but now that he was sitting right in front of me, he was as strange to me as any other man, and I didn't know what to do with myself. I wanted to escape him and his eyes and hers. I wanted him to leave. I was tired after all the hours I'd spent waiting, angry at him and at my mother for not telling me what he looked like, that he looked nothing like the picture in Grandma's photo album.

I had wanted to make my feelings clear about them tricking me into thinking he was someone other than who he was, but instead I crept behind her on the sofa and lay there crying. I'd thought that all men and boys were dark-haired like my friends in preschool and all their dads, and all girls and women were light-haired like us, and when he didn't look like that, I couldn't do anything but hide and cry. I knew it was wrong and I should stop, but I couldn't. I thought my crying might lead to him never coming back, and I suppose that's what I wanted – to never feel this disappointed again.

In the beginning they often asked me about the meaning of food in my life. The question is supposed to get you talking about it, perhaps so you'll be able to talk about it in the outside world as well. That's how I thought about it at the time. Just like I used to imagine darkness and light and that I belonged to the darkness, I imagined that those who shared my problems lived a kind of subterranean existence, detached from everything else.

They said it wasn't true, everything was one and the same, or so they claimed, and I would have to learn to be in the only world there is, which I'd thought was exclusively available to other people.

Back then, when that question was posed to me, I thought food had been so important simply because food *was* important. It was obvious to me that food should be elevated in the way I thought it was elevated in our family, and I sometimes thought everyone else should be a bit more like us, people who loved food and made an effort for the sake of food.

I saw it as my cultural inheritance and a respect for nourishment in its most fundamental sense. My mother and my grandmother had many ideas about what and how to eat, they seemed to truly love and value food, but from what my mother said, I realized that my grandmother's interest in food had also varied over the years. She hadn't always been like she was with me.

As for my mother, the taste of the food or the way it was prepared had probably not always been as important as it later became. As long as I was a small child, the necessity of eating was probably what took precedence. If I had a babysitter or was home alone because there was something she needed to do, I'd still have to eat. Whatever happened, she had to see to it and she did.

But I never thought I'd be able to eat at all when she was away, because it was as if something else was taking up that space inside me. An aching discomfort that arrived the moment I realized she was going away and lingered until she returned, sometimes longer.

I couldn't eat any proper food when I was home alone. All I wanted was the candy and cookies that came in the mail from Grandma and that I'd stashed under my bed. When winter had come to its end, she'd send me spring's first snowdrops wrapped in a bit of wet kitchen towel, and during the rest of the year, she'd send me May flowers, a five-kronor note, or a comic book or funny card, and often she would include a tasty treat. Freshly baked sugar dreams or a licorice pipe or a chocolate bar from the tobacco shop in the high-rise apartment building closest to theirs. If she had bought something there, I could tell by the whiff of tobacco that rose up the second I opened the package.

When I'd call to thank her, which my mother had told me never to forget or fail to do, which I thought was strange because I couldn't imagine my grandmother getting angry about something like that, she'd say she would have liked to send me a bag of buns and a whole rice pudding too, if only she could.

And I'd have wanted that as well.

I longed for that rice pudding as much as I longed for my grandmother, and I missed how we ate in my grandparents' home, how she'd set the table in the dinette and call out to us, and how we'd go in and take our designated seats, then stay at the table until everyone was full and had eaten up, plus a little longer for digestion's sake. The same thing day after day without disruption. I often wished I could have moved in with them and been there instead.

—

It was so strange to me that my grandmother was my mother's mother. I fantasized about what she was like back then, and when we played house in preschool, I'd want to be the mom. We used to do this after we'd eaten the last snack of the day, which consisted of raw cauliflower and pieces of rutabaga or the pale greyish winter carrots I'd gnaw the outside off of first so that only the inside was left, sweet and crunchy and resembling a tree trunk with branches sticking out. We went outside to the sandbox where our playhouse was, and I scooped up rainwater from a puddle with a bucket and stood inside the house; I poured gravel and sand into the bucket and stirred it with a stick and watched the mixture take shape and become a soup or stew for my children, who were running around outside. And when the food was ready, I set the table using sticks as cutlery and called out to the others, my husband and my children. Sometimes it took a while for them to come, especially if some were pretending to be older brothers or sisters who didn't want to come home. I told them to have a seat and dished up the food from my bucket.

In our games, that sort of thing was left to the mothers, because that's how it was in our real lives. The mothers came home with shopping bags from the grocery store, the one that had closed more than once because of robbery; they cooked food and shouted out the windows for the children to come in when it was ready. That was how it was supposed to be. Their voices echoed between the buildings and the children flew like birds to their nests and the playground emptied.

—

Sometimes kids might be allowed outside again after they'd eaten, but usually not. Usually the day ended at their dinnertime. I'd stay awhile with some older kids who'd still be in the park. There was another girl who also used to be outside when everyone else was inside eating, presumably because she was years older, as well as some guys who'd turn up around that time because they knew she'd be there. I wasn't with them, really, but more on the sidelines, while they played their games, which were so unlike ours.

I'd listen to them from my seat on a swing, gazing up at the sky between the buildings and in their direction when they weren't looking. The girl had curly hair and round eyes like the doll my mother used to talk about having as a child, the one she forgot outside one day and it melted in the sun. In the afternoons this girl was like a mother to us younger ones, a kind mother, but in the evening the boys would come looking for her and then she'd be with them. A thrill coursed through me each time they came riding on their motorcycles and everything set off between them, the way they'd go between fighting and shouting and cuddling.

There was never anyone else in the park at that hour; the adults on their way to the shop would walk around the park instead of through it, but I don't know if it was because these kids were there or for another reason or if that's just the way it was. I've since visited that park with my own children and I noticed that the whole thing was full of large dark holes, and rats scurried across the grass this way and that, but it wasn't like that back when I was little. In my memory, rabbits had lived in those holes then.

I wished the older girl wouldn't spend her time with those guys, but I also wanted to see what she'd do with them. She'd kiss one and they'd ask her to follow them somewhere, she'd giggle and laugh and seemed to enjoy it, but often something would go wrong, and once I remember it sounded like she was crying. She screamed at them to go to hell. I didn't dare look at her and kept on swinging on my swing, looking straight ahead at the gravel and the iron gate and the brown thorn bushes and the jut of nettles stripped of their flowers.

Only when I noticed that she was making her way to me did I dare to look right at her. Her face was red and eyes tear-stung when she came over to me. Let's go, she said, taking me by the hand, and I had to jog to keep up with her. All the way she talked about how tired she was of those guys, almost as if to herself, and I didn't think anyone would be at home at her apartment either, but there was, it was just that her parents were sleeping because they had to work the night shift.

The apartment looked much like ours but it smelled strange; she signalled to me that we had to be quiet and nodded toward the next room. I could hear her parents snoring in there. We went into the kitchen and she gently shut the door behind me and looked at the big clock on the wall. You're probably super-hungry, huh? she said, and filled water into a saucepan and put it on the stove.

She was even more beautiful indoors, without anyone else around and without the baggy denim jacket she wore when we were in the park. I could see her breasts under her shirt when she reached for a high shelf and took down the macaroni, which she poured into the pot and boiled for us. Now all we have to do is wait three minutes, she said. She asked where my mom was, and I said, She's working, I think, and then I watched as she took the pot off the heat and strained the steaming-hot macaroni into the sink before ladling it into two deep plates that looked just like the ones we had at school. Her mother had been a lunch lady before she started working at the factory.

She fetched the ketchup and took a large cheese out of the fridge and grated it using a grater; soft yellow shavings sailed down, which she told me to stir into the macaroni until they melted. Do you want more? she asked, and I shook my head because I couldn't say yes even though I wanted to, and she laughed and looked into my eyes and said, Go on, it's so yummy, you should have more. Then she dished up some more, then even more, as I stirred the macaroni with the spoon she'd given me until long threads of cheese stretched between them. I thought she looked so pleased watching me, as if she'd forgotten all about the park and those guys.

We were standing at the counter eating, it was hot and sweet, and I thought she was looking at me as if I were a little baby bunny she'd found in the playground and was now going to take care of. After we'd eaten up the macaroni, she walked me home. The park was empty and I remember wishing those guys would never return, but I knew it was in vain. I walked by her side and tried to compel myself to open my mouth and tell her there were probably other people she could hang out with instead. But I didn't say anything.

—

I asked my mom if we could have cheese on our macaroni too, but there was something about it she didn't like. If she joined me at mealtime, she might make boiled artichokes if they were in season, beets with herb salt or platters of cottage cheese, boiled eggs and cut-up raw vegetables, but often I'd be the only one eating dinner. She'd read the paper and drink her tea with biscuits or rusk or a sandwich.

I'd sit at the big white table in the kitchen or on the parquet floor in the living room and eat, in front of the television, which was white like everything else in our apartment and stood on a white-painted stand on wheels, or on the French balcony with the door wide open so I could look out at the carpet rack, the trees on the slope, and the high-rise building beside and feel the air from outside. I ate potatoes with herb salt, rice and corn with light margarine, rice with fish balls in lobster sauce, rice and fish sticks with soy, and corn on the cob.

Sometimes she would make me thin pancakes sprinkled with sugar. That was the only food I could stomach when she was away; pancakes meant she was going away and I'd be alone at home in the evening, and when I put two and two together, the very smell of them and the sight of that stack in the kitchen would make me ache. She'd make them in Grandma's cast-iron skillet before she left for work in the morning – at first the smell of frying that early in the morning was unusual – and then she'd sprinkle sugar on them and roll them up and leave them on the plate on the counter with another plate on top so they'd stay soft.

For a long time I thought I didn't dare tell her that I didn't want her to leave. I recalled it as one of those things I'd never been able to say and it vexed me, but that's not true. I'm sure I said that I wanted her to stay at home with me and I remember her replying that it wasn't possible. She had to do what she had to do for her job.

—

Once she was out the door and it had shut behind her in the stairwell, I'd put my hand on the knob and check that the door really was locked and then I went around turning on the lights in every room. I wanted to get this done while it was still light outside, or as soon as she left if it was winter and already dark when she set off, so I could imagine I was doing it only because I felt like it. After that, everything would turn eerie.

Because we lived on the ground floor, there were some windows outside of which I thought someone might suddenly be standing, but there were also doors inside the apartment that swung open by themselves and paintings whose motifs changed when it got dark in the evening. It was at the end of the row of buildings and so had windows looking out in three directions, just an ordinary rental apartment with white walls and white furniture, but when I was alone in it, something would always frighten me.

As soon as she went out – and sometimes all it took was for her to disappear into her room to work or go down to the laundry room to wash and dry our clothes – it was as if something in the room turned against me. All at once, it would become so quiet and empty that I began to imagine I was seeing or hearing things. I'd seen a witch in the hallway, and there was also something in the corridor between the rooms next to the kitchen, I thought. A presence that could only be felt, something I couldn't see with my naked eye but I knew it was there, brooding. It was waiting for me. I made sure not to go near it, and if I ever had to pass through the corridor to fetch something from my own room, I'd run as fast as I could there and back. I didn't want to be in my room anyway because, at any moment, someone might be standing outside its window.

After I'd turned all the lights on, I'd sit at the big white table in the kitchen and read or draw, and if that didn't work, I'd get up and go into the living room and walk around to see if that would dispel the unsettled feeling. I played my records, or kept the television on some of the time too, to keep me company and because the music or voices made it harder to listen for her, which I'd be doing otherwise, whether I wanted to or not.

I paid attention to every sound that came from beyond the entryway, only to realize that it wasn't her who was coming in. Our apartment was right by the building's entrance, and whenever someone came or went, I could hear the inner door swinging open and shut and the dull metallic bang of the outer door. Every time I heard it, I gasped for breath and thought it was her, and when the footsteps continued past our door and I realized it wasn't, I felt stupid for hoping she would come home sooner for some reason, but nonetheless the slightest sound would fill me with so much hope. It happened of its own accord and there seemed to be nothing I could do about it. It wasn't a matter of how long she'd be gone; the second she left, I wanted her back.

The pancakes she made for me really were very good, but they lacked the salty richness and pleasing subtle char of Grandma's, probably because she used butter whereas we only had margarine. I wanted to eat them and yet not. Mom and Grandma insisted that a person had to eat, and I thought that by not eating them I might change her mind, and she might stay home with me.

—

One evening after I'd turned on all the lights and was sitting in the living room and didn't know what else to do, I had an idea. I went into her bedroom and sat on the floor by the phone, picked up the receiver, and dialled the number Grandma had made me memorize so I could call anytime. You can call me whenever you like, she'd said, and I was overjoyed upon remembering that I could, because I knew everything would be better if I could just hear her voice on the phone.

Grandma had a sunny disposition, and when I talked to her, everything seemed more colourful and had a kind of warmth. I don't know what time it was when I called her and I can't remember if it was dark outside or not. I remember the ringing tone and being able to picture my grandmother's green telephone in front of me, the one that stood on the little green desk against the wall opposite the linen cabinet with the photographs on it, and I felt a pleasing anticipation in my body.

But when she answered, her voice sounded odd. She sounded as if she'd been woken up by the phone or she had been doing something important that my call had interrupted and she seemed surprised to be hearing from me. It didn't seem like she'd even expected me to call or had been thinking about me and how I was doing.

My, you're up late, she said, and her tone seemed to verge on angry, even though I knew she never got angry, because I knew she was just like Mom. Neither of them ever really got angry. It frightened me that she was so unlike herself on the phone. She sounded as if she'd been transformed or as if someone else had taken possession of her. She asked me how I was doing, and when I told her that my mom had gone out, she fell silent.

She was silent for a long time. I tried to think of the telephone wires running through the country instead of the tone of her voice, I thought how strange it was that she could be so far from me, and yet I could hear her breathing in my ear.

Hello, I said.

Have you eaten? she asked.

This was the first thing she said. I don't remember my reply or what we said to each other after, but I do remember that my cheeks flamed when I hung up the phone and my stomach twinged and ached even more. Had I eaten? I'm sure I had. Surely she'd put my pancakes on the counter before she left, and I'd probably tried not to eat them but then ate them anyway. It would end up that way – I'd eventually eat every single one even though I didn't want to.

—

I was afraid of sleeping on my own in my room, so I'd sleep in Mom's, close to her in her big bed. I loved sleeping like that. But eventually, I'm not quite sure when, her phone started ringing at night. I could hear the noisy signal in my dreams and it would wake me up, and when I opened my eyes in the dark, everything was suddenly strange and dangerous. What could anyone possibly want from her in the middle of the night?

I heard her say several times that she couldn't talk because I was asleep next to her. She hung up, but the phone rang again and again and she answered in a low mumble. She whispered and hissed and asked the man on the other end of the line to not to call here anymore. She said she was hanging up again, but when she did, it would ring again and I realized he wasn't going to leave her alone no matter what she said. He would not stop calling even though she'd asked him to, even though she'd said goodbye several times and had explained that she needed her sleep, that she had to get up early for work and that I was lying next to her.

I knew it was a man calling because I could hear him on the phone and she kept saying his name. I pretended to be asleep but was wide awake and trying to hear what they were saying to each other, listening to his voice and to hers right next to me. Sometimes it dissolved into small sobs that cut to the heart and sometimes there came a little whimper unlike anything I'd ever heard from her.

I'd never heard her cry before and never thought she could. She was otherwise so calm and big and strong, but during those nights it changed. It was as if he were in our house, trying to chase her down, and there was nothing I could do to make it stop.

The wall next to the bed was always cold, and I used to press myself against it to feel the coolness on my skin. It distracted me and made me a little calmer. I was quiet and lay perfectly still so she wouldn't notice that I was awake, and at the same time I wanted her to notice me so everything would stop. When she did not, I pressed myself harder against the wall until it felt like I was becoming one with it.

And each time, it took forever for her to get up and pull the phone cord out of the jack in the wall by the bed. After that it would be quiet, but I couldn't fall asleep because I was wondering if, since he couldn't call, he was going to show up at our home instead. I had no idea who he was, but I knew he was after her.

I was forever afraid that he would call or come to our home. I was tired because I could never sleep and felt unreal and small; I often ended up in a bad mood and when I felt one coming on I went into the kitchen to see if there was anything to eat.

I liked being there, but I also knew the kitchen was full of dangers. I could slip while standing on the kitchen counter, reaching for something on the top shelves of the cabinets, and I could hurt myself on the kitchen utensils and the stove. My mother had covered the burners so I wouldn't be scalded by boiling water or burned by a hot pan, and she had put a latch on the broom closet so I couldn't open it and cause any of what was inside to come crashing down on me.

On the wall next to the stove was a can opener with a long crank. I liked watching her guide the cans of fish balls along the blade to get them open, but it scared me too because I realized you could cut your fingers if you weren't careful. We had a pair of scissors that I thought about cutting my skin with, and in one of the drawers I found a little red plastic tool, an egg pricker, which I couldn't help but press my thumb against until the tip of the needle pushed through and a droplet of blood beaded on my skin, settling on it like a shiny insect.

Next to the can opener was a magnetic strip with a large serrated knife for cutting bread and a slightly smaller one for vegetables. I was afraid of accidentally cutting myself on the knives but also of discovering that I'd want to when I was home alone and unable to stop myself from wanting to find out how it would feel. It would be easy to cut myself in a way that would cause the blood that kept me alive to flow out, I thought, and it scared me that such thoughts could arise.

I also believed that if my life ended, so would everyone else's. I didn't know that everyone else existed in the same way as I did. I was under the impression that I was utterly alone; everything that happened only happened in my mind, and if I shut my eyes, nothing of what I'd just been looking at would still be there. Only an echoing chasm would remain.

Usually these thoughts appeared when I was tired or when it had been quiet around me for too long and something would happen to the sounds, to the sound of everything. I noticed that the softest ones, such as my mother's voice, could suddenly distort and become shrill and grating and loud. Once this got going, I couldn't get it to stop and it was so hard to explain when she'd ask me what the matter was.

I was worried this would happen and I might accidentally look for too long at a wall or into the air in front of me, as I sometimes did when I was thinking or just waiting for her to come back home or finish something she was doing that demanded her full concentration. It seemed to begin with a movement inside of what I was looking at right then, the air or the smooth white wallpaper would slacken somehow and form patterns, rippling and smoothing before my eyes, like insects swarming in the soil or grains of sand moving with the ocean waves washing in and drawing them down.

—

I was afraid of all that was surfacing inside me, but I was also afraid of what was outside, and most of all I was afraid of fear itself. When something frightened me, I'd flinch so hard and scream in a way that made everyone within eyeshot and earshot laugh. Even if they didn't want to, they couldn't help it because it looked so funny, and it made me even more vigilant and careful. I truly disliked the noises I emitted, as well as the involuntary movements I made, when I got startled. I didn't want anything like that to give me away, to reveal my fear and the fact that I wasn't a real child because I didn't have what other children had: the absence of guile in their wildness and audacity.

I wondered what it would feel like to be an adult and how much I would remember of what it was like to be a child. I wanted to remember everything and carry it with me into my future and I can recall thinking about this on the evening she brought him along to pick me up: I will never forget this. I'd been sitting by the window as usual after all the other children had gone home. I'd been looking out, expecting to see her jogging down the road from the bus stop and rushing in as she usually did, like a revelation in her garb, with her voice and all the smells I'd been longing for all day at the preschool, even though I enjoyed being there.

But instead I saw a car come to a stop and watched her get out on the passenger side. He left the driver's seat and walked over and put his arm around her shoulders, and seeing them there together I realized that life as I knew it was over. It might sound strange. I was a child, but that was what I was thinking. It didn't even take a second for me to see it, the two of them and the way they moved side by side as they traversed the sidewalk, the way she looked up at him and didn't even cast a glance at the window where I sat waiting for her.

He was the one keeping her away from me. He was the one with whom she was staying when she wasn't with me and he was the one calling our house in the night, I realized. I'd kept on pretending to be asleep each time he called, but I was always awake while it was happening, lying in the dark by the cold wall, listening to their interminable conversations and imagining myself opening my mouth to scream as if I were having a nightmare, or simply to tell her I'd heard everything. I geared up for it each time but never followed through. I stayed silent.

And I didn't speak up this time either.

When they entered the room, she hugged me as usual and faced me and said my name. This is, she then said, and spoke his name, which I decided never to take in my mouth unless I had to. Why didn't you warn me, I thought, why didn't you say anything? But I couldn't say anything. I thought his face looked disfigured; he had a large, fleshy scar across one cheek and down his neck, and when he bent down toward me, he gave off a stench that made me recoil. I didn't understand how she could stand so close to him, much less let him kiss her on the mouth and face like he did.

All the while he had his hand on her or was pulling her in for a kiss. She laughed and looked at him with her smile, which I knew I'd never be able to look at in the same way again. I thought someone had to take action – I wanted to shout for the teachers in my group, so they'd come into the hall and stop what was happening.

They needed to tell her she couldn't just come in here with him like that and we couldn't be with him, I thought, but when the teachers did appear they simply said goodbye and waved us off and we walked to his car. She put me in the back seat and buckled me in and took a seat next to him, and when he started the car and drove off I looked at the two of them sitting in front of me and realized there was nothing I could do.

Mom said he was driving us home. I looked out the car window and everything we passed looked different. He motored up the hill to the rental blocks and parked the car, and as we walked toward our building I felt that I couldn't bear the sight of it. I hated the building now and I hated our apartment when she unlocked the door and welcomed him into the hall. I hated my room and the park beyond our window where children were playing and most of all I hated being a child too, even though I didn't feel like one, and not being able to tell her she wasn't allowed to be with him.

—

I didn't want to be a child anymore, and what a burden it was to know that I had so many years of childhood left to go. Every day I sat at the big white table in the kitchen wishing for time to fly so I could become an adult and start making my own decisions. I'd been given a cookbook with recipes children could make themselves, such as flatbread rolls and baked potatoes and baked cod in foil; it was called *Now We're Cooking*, and if I was sitting there I was probably leafing through it.

I wanted to learn how to cook because it was something the adults did. The person who cooked the food was the one in control of life and such knowledge meant being able to take care of yourself, just like an adult. I read all the descriptions of how to cook various dishes and do other things in the kitchen. There were two children in every picture in the book, and in one section it said you must remember to clean up after yourself and wash the dishes when you were done, because it would make everyone else extra happy that you'd been the one to do the cooking.

I read about how to measure flour and sugar and learned how to set a timer and preheat the oven and cook some of the things I usually ate for dinner. I tried boiling eggs and rice and heating up fish balls or defrosting corn in a saucepan and I thought I could feel the adultness and self-determination in the movement of my hand each time I held a ladle or stirred something on the stove.

At my grandmother and grandfather's house, I'd once been allowed to fix supper for them, that is to say make tea and sandwiches, which I carried out on small plates to the living room, where they were watching the television news. They thought the sandwiches were tasty – salt pickles and radishes and a cheese so stinky I had to hold my breath when I sliced it – but I could tell by their faces there was something wrong with the tea. Grandad asked how I'd made it and when I told him I'd taken hot water from the tap and poured it over the tea bags, he said you couldn't do that. You had to boil the water in the kettle on the stove because there were copper deposits in the hot water pipes, which meant the water coming out of them could be dangerous to drink.

When I understood what he was saying, I felt hot and dizzy: I could have poisoned them. Not a day went by that I wasn't afraid these elderly people might die – here I was, close to killing them because I'd wanted to prepare the evening meal even though I had no idea how. That's who I was when I didn't think every single thing through, so stupid and heedless. But neither of them got angry with me, they were as kind as ever. Grandma took a bite of something from her plate, then set it aside, got up from the sofa and went back into the kitchen with me and the teacups, emptied the tea into the sink, and showed me how to fill the kettle with cold water from the tap, put it on the stovetop, and turn the heat on by twisting the knob. When it boiled, the little whistle let out a long, swaying wet sound; she let me put fresh tea bags in the cups and pour the boiling water, all the while standing behind me, at the ready with a hand resting on my shoulder.

—

Their apartment always smelled of hot food or something fresh out of the oven, and the smells would greet you in the stairwell when you arrived. Cooking took up a lot of time and space there, unlike at our home. Grandma's dishes may have been simple, rice pudding was perhaps a simple dish, but the cooking techniques were elaborate, at times verging on dramatic. At least in my eyes. Smoke and stink and clamour might arise, she'd talk herself through the ingredients and methods out loud, and would squeal if something was about to go awry and call for me or Grandad to help, I'd be handed a pot lid to hold or would stand by with a slotted spoon or clear a space for her to set one of her hot black trays on the little counter. But sometimes she just wanted me to taste a sauce or listen to what was being said on the radio.

Every Christmas she made rosettes with long, pretty rosette irons that she submerged in sizzling hot oil simmering in a pot on the stove. Sometimes she'd ask me to sit quietly at the kitchen table and not move during the process, but when I was really little, Grandad had to keep an eye on me while she was busy with that. He'd hold me tightly in his arms and I'd cling to him and ask him to take me to the stove so I could look at the oil and feel its hot fumes and the smell rising up and mingling with the faint smell of sweat from his shirt.

There would be frizzling and bubbling, and when the batter around the star-shaped iron had solidified and turned golden, she'd lift it out just as slowly and carefully, never taking her eyes off the oil. Then she'd place the steaming rosettes on a platter and, once they'd cooled, she powdered them with sugar that made the shapes look like snow crystals. As with everything else she did, she seemed so happy to be doing it. Baking, washing and cleaning, making cordial and jam or her own preserves, reading the circulars and jotting things down on the shopping list and tearing it off the roll and taking her handcart to the shopping centre across the road and then coming home and setting the kitchen table, turning on the radio in the kitchen and preparing a meal. All of it seemed fun to her or at least enjoyable in some way; she'd sing her songs and whistle as she moved through the rooms, and Grandad would sit and read in the armchair he'd built himself, or help her whenever an extra pair of hands or someone stronger and taller was needed.

~

I thought of Grandma as someone who was always at home, but until the day she retired, she'd always gone to work. She wrote about this in the responses she sent me for my school assignment to interview an older relative. When she was fourteen years old, she started as an aide in a hospital, with food and lodging as compensation, and then she'd worked for all those years, mostly as a house girl, she wrote, and she kept on working after she and Grandad got married. Because married women were expected to be at home, she decided to take a job at a laundry instead, close enough to their two-room apartment for her to walk home on her lunch break and cook for her husband and children and then go back to work. She wanted to earn her own money to do with as she pleased.

Mom had said that Grandma and Grandad were often away at important political meetings in the evenings when she was little, and I wondered if that was why everything Grandma did at home seemed so pleasant, as if it could be such a pleasure for her because she hadn't always done it, or was it related to the joy of having her own home and her own family, and food with which to feed them?

Maybe she was just happy to have me there. The first thing she asked every time I walked through their door was if I was hungry and wanted something to eat. If I said yes, she would light up, go back into the kitchen and take things out and serve something freshly arranged on a plate. If I said no, she'd take stock of me and my alleged satiety, in order to find my weak spot. There was always room for something, it was just a matter of knowing what. You do want a bite, don't you? A piece of fruit or a sandwich? How about some sour milk? You have to eat!

If I wouldn't let her feed me anything, it was as if she were at a loss and didn't know what to do with me or with herself. Not eating what she was offering seemed to almost hurt her. As I got older, it irritated me. I felt ashamed when she kept asking people who stopped by if they were hungry and wanted something to eat, even though it wasn't close to meal time and they were probably not at all hungry and certainly weren't the kind who, like us, constantly wanted to be eating.

At the same time, I felt ashamed for feeling ashamed and because I was irritated with her and felt like I couldn't breathe as she hovered around me during each of my visits, with all her questions about food, grabbing me and pinching my cheek or looking at my body and asking if I was eating enough. On a few occasions I punished her by standing by my refusal of her offerings, but as a small child I liked it. Everything she set out for me felt so warm and welcoming, and I hated when Mom came to visit and Grandma started asking what she wanted. Each time I sensed Grandma's hopes and each time Mom refused everything. For Grandma it was the beginning of a kind of negotiation, but the more she tried, the stronger Mom's defences became. I listened from the living room, hoping all the while that she would give in, that her voice would soften and I would hear her say, Yes, I'll have a taste if there's some going, since you've already gone to the trouble of cooking.

When that happened, I could hear the happiness in Grandma's steps and movements as she picked up a plate and lifted the lid off a saucepan and dished it up. And then I went to watch my mother eat at the table with the oilcloth and the radio in Grandma's little kitchen. In there, she was an anomaly. She didn't fit in Grandma and Grandad's apartment. It was as if she didn't belong at all. She rarely visited, and when she did, it was usually in the company of others, relatives or other family members, and she'd turn up last, as if she'd wanted to put off the visit for as long as possible or simply allow it not to materialize.

—

When she arrived, sometimes she'd go into the kitchen and start walking around, sort of inspecting what was there. I didn't like it when she did that and didn't want Grandma to see her. She might bend down and pull a pan out of the cupboard and take paper towels and wipe away the whitish-blue layer of grease that covered the bottom and built up in waves toward the edges, or wash the coffee cups and glasses that Grandma had already washed. She can't see, she'd whisper to me, nodding surreptitiously in Grandma's direction, but I wasn't convinced that was the case. I figured Grandma could see; she just wanted to keep the grease in the pan because it was good for frying, and her dishes didn't have to be sparkling clean.

It was strange to think that my mother actually belonged to them more than I did, because they were her parents. She was their child – Grandma had given birth to her and held her in her arms, like she used to hold me. It seemed almost unbelievable. My mother's smell deviated from all the other smells in there; it could be her physical smell or the perfume she misted herself with sometimes, or just her usual smell, of which I could never get enough. She moved around their apartment as if it were too small for her, even though it was bigger than ours, and when we ate, she seemed to secretly wrinkle her nose at Grandma's food – or did she simply want us all to understand that there was other food in the outside world, the one she resided in, food that was more special and much tastier than what we were eating?

She might talk about some spot where she'd eaten something that was so insanely good, as she put it, and this was the kind of thing she'd talk about especially often at Grandma and Grandad's. When she described food, it was as if in that moment I could see her in the place where she'd eaten it, as if I could be there with her for a spell. She would talk and move her hands and form her lips as if those flavours were once again on her tongue, and sort of tempted us with her story about them, or about what she'd learned about food, its origins and how it was to be handled. It could be that she'd been given something to eat that she'd never tasted before, which she could not have imagined would be as good as it was, or that she'd been instructed to cook a dish in a way that was new to her. Sometimes she told Grandma that next time the shopping needed doing, she'd go with her to the grocery store down at the shopping centre to show Grandma all the things that were there that she didn't yet know about and tell her how to use them, things that had never previously been available and were unknown to Grandma and Grandad.

My grandmother did not eat meat, but she often made meat dishes for my grandfather. Pyttipanna hash with pickled beets and fried eggs, pan-fried beef with fried onions, kalops beef stew with boiled and mashed potatoes and smoke-cured loin of pork with rice and stewed spinach or steamed cauliflower. She served him these dishes but only ate the sides herself, and I did the same.

One day in the middle of the summer holidays, when onions and carrots were still sprouting from the earth and it was light until late in the evening, Grandma said she had to go into town and see the doctor. I remember her saying not to worry, but it seemed worrying and I wished she wouldn't go. She'd never left us before, and it was so strange to watch her getting ready, hanging her bag over her shoulder, and putting pink shimmer on her lips. Everything proceeded slowly, as if I could do something to stop it, but I couldn't think what that might be.

She looked like a completely different person when she left. She hugged me and stepped across the threshold and out the door, down the porch steps, and off along the garden path. My stomach dropped and ached as she disappeared from sight behind the hedge that framed our property and went on her way to the bus stop. Whelp, Grandad exclaimed, bringing his hands together in the air with a clap and patting me on the head. I guess you'll be making the kalops for me today, he said, laughing and giving my shoulder a little shake. I felt everything inside me shift. I was so happy and at the same time so nervous about being assigned such an important task, I couldn't think about anything else. I'd be cooking the day's main meal for my grandfather. I was finally grown-up, or at least about to be.

The community garden cottage was a bit outside the town where Grandma and Grandad lived. You entered from the road through a gate with tall white pillars; in the middle of the area was the grassy common with the grocery store on one side and a flagpole in the middle, and from there ran narrow paths, all named after garden trees, plants, and shrubs, in alphabetical order. Astrachan, barberry, cypress, daphne, everlasting flower. Rows of cottages with no basement but with gardens, outhouses, and sheds, and beyond them, the sea.

The grocery store had a kiosk where you could buy loose candy that the fat cashier would pluck for you with tongs from the row of small plastic boxes at eye level and drop into a small paper bag. Once, when Mom was visiting and went with me to the store to look for something she was missing in Grandma and Grandad's pantry, she laughed all the way back to the cottage about the way one of the salesladies inside had pronounced a word. I think it might have been *bacon*, which the woman called *bason pork*. I loved it when my mother laughed like that, a wild sort of giggle all her own, but I also really liked the dialect that everyone spoke there and that was particularly strong in some. Mom didn't like it one bit, because it reminded her of when she'd lived there as a young girl, and my grandmother would say it was always such a surprise when she met cute little girls who'd open their mouths and out would come a bleating so rough and crude she could hardly hear what they were saying.

I can picture them now, how they'd shake and appear to be getting full-body chills from that dialect of theirs. I thought it was warm and vibrant, and the words seemed to be lilting alongside a gentle burr. I loved that it sounded so special and different, a constant reminder that I was actually in that place simply because of how people spoke and the reverberation of it around me.

On the lawn in front of the little shop, a bun party was held every summer; freshly baked cardamom buns and wheat buns and cinnamon rolls were handed out to everyone who came, and at the end of the summer it was Coca-Cola day, when a big Coca-Cola truck would drive into the area with young people in Coca-Cola clothes setting up games and competitions where we children could win beach chairs and tracksuits or lie-on floats and inflatable pools. Everything was made of red plastic with the wavy white Coca-Cola letters on it, and even if you didn't win anything, you'd be given a Coca-Cola and a token to take home, maybe a baseball cap and a frisbee or stickers, things like that. We didn't drink pop, so I never had, and I hadn't liked it at all the few times I'd sampled it at someone else's house, so I'd give mine away to someone else.

—

The bus stop lay steps beyond the neighbourhood gates. Right as my grandmother had set off in that direction, my friend came along on his bike; it had thick tires and training wheels and a pennant just like on the bike Grandma and Grandad had given me. He stopped on the grass in front of the steps to the porch and asked if I was coming along to the hut. Off the path that led to the beach and the community garden's jetty was an overgrown deserted lot behind a grove of trees, with a dilapidated cottage we played in every day. It was the last lot on the street at the far end of the community garden, and we called it the hut because the big kids had told us to, so no grown-up would know we were playing in an abandoned building. The windows were broken and the roof had started to sag in places. There was an armchair inside with the springs sticking out, the cupboards were full of pill cases with remnants of old medicine, and the floor of the cottage was covered with broken glass and piles of empty cookie wrappers and coconut-chocolate-ball packages and plastic casing from sausages, headcheese, and paté. A hermit once lived there, someone who'd retreated from everything. It was as if there were a warm darkness around the broken armchair and I thought about how good it must feel to sit there and eat and watch television isolated from the outside world.

When I told him I couldn't go with him, he was surprised. What did I have to do that was so important? And I told him that Grandma had gone into town and I had to stay home and make dinner for Grandad. He laughed. You can't cook dinner, can you? he said, then cycled off toward the empty lot with the cottage. I felt a pang of longing, but no more. I was used to being able to help out a bit from time to time, but it had never been like this – this was first time I'd been assigned a task that was actually meaningful. But why hadn't she given me any instructions?

I wondered how to go about it. Apart from the meat for the kalops, the hardest thing would be to reach everything I needed that was kept up high, I thought, and to get the heavy iron pot out of the cupboard. I could ask Grandad to help me, but that didn't feel right because he'd asked me to cook. I should be able to manage on my own, all of it.

The kitchen in the cottage was so small it could hardly be called a kitchen. It had green-painted walls and cupboards, a cork mat on the floor and a small window above the counter through which Grandma, while doing the dishes, could look out at the beauty bush growing right outside, like a boundary between us and the neighbouring plot. It was more of a kitchenette really, two adults could probably stand side by side in there, if they were barely moving. It was like a small cooking closet full of mingling smells and jostling, while cooking was going on but also when nothing was on the stove. The smells came from the metal bucket in the cabinet under the sink, where the compost was, from the chamber pot that stood behind it and from the thin blue-and-white-striped dish-cloth that Grandma boiled again and again so it would last all summer. There was also the smell of damp soil from the enamel colander that usually sat on the little bench with radishes, summer squash, lettuce, and bunches of spinach from the garden. There was a refrigerator filled with all sorts of leftovers, saved carrot greens, buckling and pickled herrings, clay jars of drippings that had been collected, and cans of beer from which Grandma would take two for the pair of workers who came to collect the barrels from the privy. Seeing them drag the big, heavy barrels filled with our stinking remains through the garden and hoist them onto the big vehicle never stopped being strange. If it was sunny, they'd usually sit over by the outhouse in a secluded corner of the plot and drink the beer there, far enough away so as not to disturb her, while still being able to respond when she spoke to them, shouting or making a bit of small talk from a distance, and each time I wished they'd finish up soon because their beards and booming voices frightened me and I knew I wouldn't dare use the privy while they were there, even if I needed to go.

The beer cans in the fridge were part of a system I hadn't observed anywhere but at Grandma's house. On the evening before Christmas Eve, right after we arrived at their home, I'd be sent along with her to the tobacconist two buildings over to buy a two-hundred-gram chocolate bar, which she took out later that night and hung by a gift ribbon on the doorknob with a note that said *To the Newsboy* before she went to bed, and on New Year's Eve she gave freshly baked fruitcakes and azaleas to the caretaker and the Finnish girls who cleaned the stairwell. These were the most important tasks of her year. It was important never to forget any of this; we must show our gratitude to everyone who performed the necessary work without which we would not be able to manage, the people all around who simply carried on like an invisible machine, and it was made clear that I was to follow suit.

I was to be grateful that we had food and someone to take care of our waste and grateful that the life I'd been given was so simple and orderly. I was to curtsy and shake hands and call the neighbours Mr. and Mrs. when we went visited them and remember to say thank you. Once when I forgot, Grandad roared that I was to say thank you every time anything was put in my hand, even if it was just the butter knife he was passing me at breakfast, and I thought there must be more he wasn't mentioning, more I should do to earn everything I'd been given in addition to my fortunate position in time and space.

—

Hanging on a hook on the wall above the stove in the kitchenette was an old waffle iron with long handles that Grandma took out once a summer to make waffles for a party for all the children on the street. And in the cupboard were jars of cookies she'd take out when it was her turn to invite the other old ladies in the neighbourhood over for coffee. They took turns each week – there were usually at least eight kinds: oatmeal cookies, caramel cookie cuts, raspberry thumbprint cookies, sugar dreams, Brussels biscuits, chessboard cookies, farm biscuits, and

Finnish sticks. She baked in batches and kept them highest up on a shelf I couldn't reach no matter how hard I tried.

Some of the neighbouring aunties also served cinnamon swirls or Danishes, and there was always lemonade or milk for me; I was the only child at the aunties' coffee parties, and if there was milk it would be the creamy kind, usually lukewarm from the summer heat or an old-fashioned refrigerator so I couldn't drink even a single sip but had to sit there with the full glass in front of me, a lone fly navigating the rim and periodically diving down to touch the surface. I would sit with Grandma, on her lap for the first few years, then beside and leaning against her when I got bigger, and every time the buns and cakes and cookies were set out, she'd look down at me and roll her eyes and say loud enough for the auntie we were visiting to hear: My, what a party we've been invited to!

I'd nod vigorously and smile and it was often sincere; I liked the farm cakes at least and the smooth wheat buns with cardamom in the dough that I got at some people's houses, but there was so much that made my stomach turn. I couldn't eat the things that were too sugary or fatty or had an insipid or perfumed taste, the bitter almond cookies and the mazarins or the Danishes and cinnamon rolls with almond paste. I couldn't eat cream cakes or tarts, which made me feel ashamed because everybody loved those; such baked goods were the best of the best and you were meant to show your appreciation when they were carried in and placed in front of you.

I would hack at the pound-cake base with my spoon, smear the cream around my plate, and try to quickly slide my piece to Grandma when no one was looking. I never stopped missing my mother and, had she been there, I imagined she wouldn't have wanted the cake either. I remembered what she'd told me about her childhood, how she'd been made to sit at the table and finish what was on her plate even though she couldn't, how once she'd sat there for so long she wet herself, and I couldn't understand why Grandma and Grandad, who were only ever kind, would do such a thing to her.

I remember Grandad eating his breakfast at the table in the room as usual that morning after Grandma had gone into town. He ate indoors even if the weather was nice because he'd spend most of the day working out in the garden anyway, training his berry bushes and beans or weeding and digging new strawberry and potato patches or working in his shed, but she and I liked to sit on the porch, next to the pots of sweet peas, clematis, and begonias she'd hung there and the ornamental grapevine that climbed from the beds of earth up the railing and over the roof.

I was waiting for Grandad to finish reading the newspaper and for the morning to pass so the time for me to do what I had to do would come. My big task. Dinner was usually eaten at one o'clock and it was probably important to stick to the schedule, I thought, because if I didn't make it in time, it would be as if I hadn't in fact made dinner. Eventually he came out and said he'd be working in the shed awhile. He'd had a job as an upholsterer during his time with the railroad, he owned lots of tools he kept in the shed, and he'd still reupholster the odd piece of furniture or make something. Whatever the case, he spent a lot of time in there and I didn't think much about it because I was usually busy with my friends and the hut and a little crooked weeping birch tree in one corner of the yard. I used to climb it and use the curve of a large branch as a table when Grandma brought me my snack or supper while I was up there. But I can imagine that Grandad was going to do some turning or planing in the shed that day, and when he disappeared inside it, I dragged the stepstool from the hall into the kitchenette.

The first thing I noticed was that my grandmother had left the cast-iron pot on the stove after cleaning and burning it off the day before. She'd set it out for me, I thought. I felt an immediate sense of relief. I'd been dreading that the most. Then I set to work. I began by washing the dish and cup that Grandad had left in the sink. The water was soft, not like what came out of the faucet at home, not as wet, however strange it was that water could be wet in different ways. A stale smell came from the sink, metal and a lingering whiff of urine that I tried to put out of my mind, as if thinking about other things could stop the scent particles from releasing their substances.

Once I'd rinsed the dish and cup, I took the plastic cutting board down from its hook behind the dish rack and the carving knife from the drawer. I didn't give a single thought to its shiny sharp edge, because even that couldn't distract me from the task ahead. I'd been at the store with Grandma when she bought the meat and I'd seen her put it in the meat compartment in the refrigerator. I took out the package and weighed it in both hands before opening it, peeling off the waxed white paper and placing the meat on the cutting board.

Shoulder clod is my guess, now that I know a bit more about meat and what different cuts look like. I do eat meat now sometimes, but back then it was foreign to me. In the centre of it was the sawed-through white bone; I leaned forward and sniffed it, and the smell of marrow made my stomach turn. I dropped the knife and, after climbing down from the stool to pick it up, I stood for a moment in the open doorway and breathed in the air in the hallway outside the kitchenette, all the cottage's other smells of paper and dust and old sun-bleached cloth.

Then I climbed onto the stool again and took fresh hold of the meat. It was just meat. It was going to be kalops. I just had to endure. It was slimy to the touch, and when I cut the shaft of the bone out with the knife, blood started seeping. I placed the little marrow bone in the pot as I'd seen my grandmother do and drove the knife through the meat like I thought I'd seen her do, cutting thick slices first and then bits, and I tried to keep my fingertips out of the way like she had shown me.

The meat juice and water glossed my fingers. I could have cut them off like little pork sausages, but I held my hand like a claw. Though the knife was sharp, I still struggled to slice through the membranes and the sinew and the fat. The blood spilled onto the cutting board and spread, filling the many notches left by the knife's edge in the plastic. My mother had once been a vegetarian like my grandmother, we never ate meat at home, and when I saw it like this, up close, all I could think about was the animal it once had been, the warm creature that made sounds and moved around and had a smell, and that I thought reminded me of myself. I could have petted it or put my arms around it and felt its body so close to mine. It upset me that it hadn't been allowed to live. I'd seen cows in a pasture once, and I'd seen a movie about a slaughterhouse, in which pigs were lined up in a row and cut open, their guts and intestines spilling out, and even though I tried not to think about it, it was hard to keep going with the knife. I held my breath as I cut up the last of the meat, and what was left of the piece I wrapped up in the waxed paper and put back in the fridge.

—

I dropped the bloody cubes of meat into the pot, which was black with a greasy shine inside, and then I took out the celery and onion. I knew that chopping an onion was no mean feat either; I had watched my grandmother wipe tears away with the corner of her plaid apron, and I'd heard her mention how chewing a piece of crispbread or running the faucet while chopping could make it easier. Still, I hadn't thought it would be as difficult as it was. My eyes burned and tears rolled down my cheeks. I bit into some crispbread, but it didn't help, and after a while it was as if I were being swept along a bit and I started actually crying because I realized that no one would be able to tell the difference – if Grandad came in, I could just say it was nothing, I was chopping onions for the kalops.

My tears tasted salty and sweet. I thought of Grandma, who was at the doctor, and even though I was in fact busy with the onions, sometimes when I cried I wanted to cry more and I couldn't see an end to my sadness. It was like a tidal wave washing over me and dragging me out and away. If only Grandma and Grandad weren't so old that they might die, I thought as I lifted the cutting board like I'd seen Grandma do and scraped the onion into the pot using the knife's shiny blade. If only my mother didn't have to work so much. I wondered where she was and what she was doing and if she could at least send me a card or a letter soon. Why wasn't she writing to me?

With this thought, I stopped crying. I turned the knob until I heard a click inside the stove and the electric yellow light came on and then I poured in two cups of water like I'd seen Grandma do, from the little white cup with pink roses and a worn gold rim. Then I stood on the steps by the stove and stirred the water with a wooden ladle. Bits of onion and meat circled around the marrow bone that lay still in the centre; I stirred and stirred and stared into the vortex, stopped stirring and watched as the bottom of the pot heated up and little bubbles took shape and rose through the water. But something was missing. I climbed down and dragged the stool along with me to the other end of the small kitchen, to an ornamented wooden shelf lined with small jars. There was a green glass jar with a dark teak lid containing dried green leaves, and a similar one with small round white grains.

Then I remembered that I needed to add a carrot to the pot, but it wasn't enough, even with the carrot and the spices it looked nothing like kalops, and I felt my heart speed up and my hands tremble as I stirred the pot with the ladle. I didn't understand what I'd done wrong. Why couldn't it just work, why wasn't it turning out the way I wanted?

Then I realized I needed to wait. Grandma would start her stew in the morning to have it ready in time for dinner, and I'd heard her often say the kalops needed time, so maybe if I waited it would sort itself out. I wondered what would happen if she didn't come back or if it turned out she was sick, what the rest of the summer would be like and who would take care of me then. Would it just be my grandfather and me or would I have to stay with my other relatives? My mother had said that if she were to die, I'd go live with them. Why not with Grandma and Grandad, I'd asked, and she said they were too old, they didn't have the energy for a small child. But they could manage for a whole summer, I thought. I looked at the bay leaves and peppercorns floating around in the pot like driftwood on a tiny sea and I pictured Grandma, her hospital visit complete, now standing in the square filling perfectly ripe peaches into a bag while anticipating taking her seat on the bus and making her way back to us. But I knew that wasn't necessarily the case.

～

I felt tired. My hands were wet and spongy from being in contact with so much water, I was sweating, it was hard work climbing up and down the stepstool and shoving it around the kitchenette. I kept checking the pot, but nothing was happening. I turned up the heat on the stove to get it to simmer, gave the pot a stir, and followed the bubbles with the wooden spoon, and somehow time must have passed while I stood there stirring because the stew thickened and became fragrant. I climbed down from the stool once more and took some potatoes out of the big wooden box at the bottom of the pantry. The patterned paper bulged in places on the shelves, it smelled of coarse-ground coffee and damp biscuits and something a little mouldy in there, and on the edges of the shelves were beautiful strips of white-cotton-embroidered edging affixed with drawing pins in various colours. Grandma had let me help peel winter potatoes a few times that summer, so it wouldn't be difficult; I loved the sound the peeler made when you moved it up and over the earthy lumps. I picked off the chubby sprouts protruding from the eyes of the potatoes – I knew that's what the holes they came out of were called – and I cut off the green parts that were said to be toxic.

I threw the scraps into the metal bucket to be carried out to the compost where it would become soil and then I could finally get on with the potato peeler. I kept my hand under the narrow jet of water and enjoyed watching the wet strips of peel drop into the sink one by one. But the peeler was sharp and sliced a piece of the skin off the hand holding the potato as I was changing my grip, right below my thumb. The blood pushing through turned the thin flap of skin red. I rinsed it off but it kept coming and I kept rinsing and rinsing the blood until I remembered that my grandmother had taught me to apply pressure to a wound if I cut myself. The same went for a big accident, you'd apply a pressure bandage to stop the bleeding. I wanted to go to Grandad in his shed but thought it best not to, what I wanted was to go to him and say that the food was ready, not that I'd hurt myself, so I took some sheets from the roll of paper towels on the wall and pressed the flap of skin as hard as I could for a long time, until it stopped bleeding and I could finish the potatoes.

After I put them in a pot of water and the pot on the stove, there was nothing to do but wait. When Grandad was little, his parents and several of his siblings had died, and Grandma's closest sister was also dead. I didn't know how I'd cope if my mother died. I quickly prayed for this not to happen. The God I prayed to was an all-seeing, all-powerful God who could make terrible things stop or make them happen, as well as bring people closer together or further apart. He could take and give back, depending on what he thought was right, and because he was all-seeing and all-knowing, he could see me now in the kitchenette and in the evenings as I lay there thinking about my father and my mother and praying for her return.

—

The steam from the meat rose toward me as I stood on the stool in the heat of the stove. I'd heard that God would protect me if I prayed. The neighbours' daughter had said so. She was very kind and beautiful and glad to talk, and she'd given me a little evening prayer laminate, which I kept on my bedside table and read every night. If I felt lonely I could always pray, she said, because God was everywhere and in everyone, and if it felt like he wasn't, he'd appear if only you prayed hard enough. I didn't understand why no one else had ever told me that, how simple it was, but she was a priest or was going to be a priest, and was the only person I knew who knew anything about God. I assumed that everyone was telling her the same thing they did me, that God was just a word used to fool people and oppress them. When I asked my mother if she believed in God, she'd said she believed in goodness, that there was good in everyone, and when I asked my grandmother, my grandfather laughed out loud and my grandmother said, No siree. When she worked as a hospital aide, she'd been the one to hold the children who were going to be baptized by the priest, the ones who needed to be baptized because they might not survive, and each time the priest had grabbed her breasts and she hadn't been able to do anything because she was holding a baby and she couldn't say anything either because it was the occasion of the child's baptism.

I thought about this while searching a kitchen drawer for Grandma's cake tester. I knew that the potatoes and the meat should feel about the same to the touch, because I'd heard her say that once when her hands were full and she'd asked Grandad to check them. The meat had gone tender and the smell of kalops had begun to rise from the pot, filling the kitchenette and the hall and the next room, although I hardly dared leave the stove during the cooking process. I liked standing there and following its transformation. I peered into the pot, surprised to find that it resembled what I thought it should; the water had taken on the colour of the meat and thickened into a shiny gravy, the carrot pieces had a yellowish sheen, and the onion was no more than a scattering of pale streaks.

I poked a potato with the metal stick and it slid right through. Then I turned off the burner and went out to the shed to summon Grandad. I don't remember what the inside of his shed looked like, but I can see him in front of me, holding a large planer in his hands, and how he seemed hesitant when I said the food was ready, like he had more to do and didn't want to come in and eat just yet. Or was it something else? I felt uncertain. The kalops is ready, I said, the potatoes are hot. Let's eat, Grandad. I felt like I practically had to beg him, and then he laughed and set the planer aside. He wrapped his big hand around mine when I held it up to him, and we left the shed together. We crossed the lawn and walked past the hammock and garden furniture over by the weeping birch. Let's see what you've been up to, he said. Yes, I said. I kept my eyes on the lawn and treaded carefully because somewhere there I'd stepped on a hornet the previous summer. He'd come running and picked me up and carried me into the house, Grandma had run after us from the garden patch, and when we got into the room he'd laid me over an armchair and taken my foot and sucked the hornet's stinger and all the poison out of it. Several neighbours turned up to ask what was going on because my screams had resounded throughout the neighbourhood, and I remember hearing them talking to each other about an old lady who had died because of a hornet a couple of summers before.

—

I looked up at Grandad, and his nostrils widened in the air. Smells like food, he said, and I was glad because I knew he liked it when it did. When Mom said it smelled like food, for example in the stairwell of our building, it was a bad thing, but when Grandad said it smelled like food, it was something good. He even enjoyed the smell that filled the apartment like a fog whenever Grandma made pancakes or burger patties and he'd look happy to be sitting down at a table, clapping his hands together with a bang before eagerly inspecting what had been laid out for him and digging in.

We'd eat dinner inside the cottage even when the weather was nice, unless it was Midsummer's Eve or during a waffle party or something similar. Grandad sat down at the table and gave me an amused and playful look. Well, he said, let's see what kind of tasty dish you've rustled up. I went into the kitchen and climbed onto the stool. I'd put his plate right next to the stove and reached for the handle of the wooden ladle that was in the pot, but somehow I lost my balance and slapped the ladle with my hand and it flew into the air, splattering kalops on my shirt and shorts and on the wall and floor behind.

How typical for this to have gone well right until the end. I scurried down and grabbed my grandmother's dishcloth, which I usually didn't want to be near. Now I was throwing myself at it, using it for wiping up, then rinsing it out, then wiping some more. I'd let my guard down too soon and been far too sure of myself and now God wanted to punish me or just remind me not to take anything for granted. I heard Grandad humming in the other room and hoped he wouldn't come in and see the mess. I tore a sheet off the roll of paper towels on the wall, ran it across the stains on my clothes. Then I started from the top: I climbed onto the stool and ladled the kalops onto the plate, which I carried over and held out for him.

He stopped humming and fell silent. I wondered if I should've riced the potatoes with that big ricer Grandma kept in a drawer. Then I looked at Grandad. He was sitting up straight, fists lightly clenched and resting on either side of the plate as usual, then he straightened up a little more while looking down at the plate. He seemed delighted. This was what he always did, anything could have been on the plate, I suppose, but then he glanced up at me without a word. His mouth was open but nothing was coming out of it, his jaw had dropped. Then he turned his eyes back to his plate. Did Grandma make this before she left? he asked. No, I said, I made it, and I felt a rush.

With a hint of suspicion, he picked up his fork and jabbed it into a piece of meat in gravy, let his knife slide along the threads that had taken on a greyish-purple sheen, dragged the fork around the kalops, and put it in his mouth. He chewed and smiled and swallowed and then broke out in laughter; he slapped his knee and laughed even more and reached out his big hand, speckled and gnarled, and put it on my shoulder and gave it a shake, I remember exactly how it felt, and then he removed it to caress my cheek, used his thumb to wipe something that seemed like kalops from my forehead. Well, I'll be, he said. You've made a kalops just like your grandmother's! Who'd have thought that you'd cook dinner. He looked at me with his mouth open again. I didn't understand a thing. I waited for him to explain, but he turned his attention to his plate and looked at it. He picked up the salt shaker and shook it a few times over his food, the salt falling onto it like white rain, then he speared another piece of meat along with a piece of potato and let the fork slide around until that bite was coated in the shiny gravy.

I didn't know that kalops needed thickening, and even if I had, I wouldn't have known how to make a roux; neither did I know that you were supposed to start by melting butter in the pot and putting in the onions and carrots first before adding the meat and letting it all brown and then adding in the water, but maybe it didn't make much difference to the end result, and anyway he didn't say anything. He really did seem to like it. He took another bite and looked at me and laughed again. Then he put down his fork and asked if I was going to eat. I fixed myself a plate of boiled potatoes and gravy and carrots and carefully carried it to the table, and as we sat opposite each other eating he said several times how good it was and how amazed he was that I could cook even though I was so young.

~

It was nightfall by the time Grandma returned. A large swarm of gnats was buzzing around her as she came up the garden path. I was sitting on the porch drawing pictures for the book about my summer vacation that I was working on and Grandad was in my room, the small room with two narrow single beds and a nightstand between them where Grandma used to have a rest in the evening, so that I wouldn't feel too lonesome. She gave me a hug and I waited for her to tell me about her visit to the city, but right then Grandad came out on the porch and told her I'd made him kalops for dinner. She smiled. You're telling tales! she said. No, it's true, Grandad said. Grandma looked at me: *You* made kalops?, and I nodded. She didn't seem to know whether to laugh or something else, and Grandad said he'd only been joking when he'd asked me to make dinner. I felt stupid for not realizing it was a joke, but also proud that I'd done it and done it so well. Grandma pulled me onto her lap and stroked my hair. My little darling, she said, what a marvel! She gazed at me awhile and put her arms around me and then she started laughing and laughed for a long time.

For the rest of that summer I'd hear her telling all the neighbours and everyone else we knew who stopped by for a coffee that I had cooked dinner for Grandad when she was in town. They were surprised and laughed at her way of telling the story and told me how good I was, bent down and touched me and looked into my eyes and said they'd never heard of such a thing, what a good girl. At first my cheeks would burn each time and I'd try to get closer to my grandmother in order to disappear behind her legs, but after a few times it was as if a flame was lit inside me. The aunties would ask about me and she'd tell me how brilliant it was that I knew how to do so many things and for spending so much time there over the holidays. And when my mother came to visit or pick me up, my grandmother would tell her how good I'd been, that I hadn't missed her and never complained, I'd been nothing but kind, never got angry or sad about anything.

I was used to hearing adults talk about me, when they knew I was listening and when they didn't think I was.

I still catch myself wondering what Grandma and Grandad would have thought of my rice pudding. The taste of it, but also the fact that I'd made it at all and wanted to make it again and again. What would they have thought about the delight I took in the idea of a life that would be about nothing more than reviving my memories of what we used to eat? Was this what they'd envisioned for me? That such a big part of me would still be lingering with them in their kitchen and dinette, even though I was living my life in a different place and in a completely different way?

I wonder what they would have thought about who I'd become. They had such high hopes for how the future would unfold, but they didn't talk about my future specifically. Unlike the other adults I knew, my mother, the man she insisted on seeing, and their friends and colleagues with whom we were often at parties or the pub never expressed any opinions or hopes about it; they just seemed to think the important thing was to be nice and do the right thing as they themselves did and as their own parents had done, at least my grandmother's parents, who were special because they'd been so kind to their children and had not beaten them. Grandma's father had been beaten so often when he was little that he never touched her and her sisters, and she talked about it often, how unusual it was and how lucky they were to have parents like that. But she also wrote to me that she wished they'd been able to invite the headmaster over for dinner, so she would have had the chance to go to secondary grammar school after elementary school. That's how it was back then, she wrote. I wanted so much to continue my education, but it was out of the question for a working-class girl.

When I read her answers on the page now, I see that she'd spelled almost every word correctly, and where she hadn't, she'd caught herself and changed it afterwards. She must have sat at her kitchen table with the lined A4 paper in her hands and read them through one last time before folding up the sheets and putting them in an envelope and mailing it to me. At the bottom of the first page is a dark grease stain.

She wrote that she'd never liked eating meat. When she was a child, she preferred to go outside and pull a turnip out of the ground whenever meat was being served, she wrote. She often returned to the fact that this was what she had done.

When she said meat, I think she meant pork – roast pork and boiled pig's feet or offal and tongue – but perhaps at some point they had neck or shank or some other front quarter of beef that had to be boiled for a long time for it to become tender. Had she been served roast veal and meatballs with gravy as a child, it might have been different. Then she might actually have liked meat, but the fact that she refrained from eating it was also consistent with the image I had of her. She loved animals and children and was so kind, as if she couldn't get angry or be mean, but she also spoke up when she thought something was wrong and would talk about the importance of doing so. On the bus, she would leave her seat to have a word with parents who were scolding their children too harshly or were being too rough with them, and when the neighbours made a racket, she would get Mom to go ring the doorbell. And if we passed the square on a weekend when the chairman of the nationalist local patriotic party was speaking there, she'd go over and ask him to keep quiet.

Perhaps rice pudding had such a prominent place in her kitchen because it was a meat-free dish that Grandad also liked. I could imagine her with her long braids running to the turnips and grabbing them right out of the black earth, as she'd so often recounted. I thought it was like a rebellion against that time, her daring to refuse meat, but even when she was a child, eating certain foods and avoiding others was a way of differentiating yourself from the masses. To choose what you want to eat and what you don't is to be above it all, and it was that way a hundred years ago as well, or maybe even more so? I didn't think of her as the ascetic type because I so often saw her pop candy or some leftovers or whatever into her mouth, but maybe saying no to something came as a relief. To not have to eat everything that was put in front of her, but actually be able to defend herself against her voracious hunger at least in one respect.

Or was hers not a voracious hunger?

Am I simply talking about myself?

It's hard to explain this to someone who doesn't know. It's hard to talk about it with someone who hasn't felt it themselves, or seen it with their own eyes, because so many people simply can't believe it's true. They don't want it to be. It's too irritating or too painful that some of us can't handle the most basic aspect of existence, that which should be a source of joy, vitality, and satisfaction.

But it is also difficult for me to know what this is. I imagine that so much revolved around food, but maybe this was true only for me. This relationship may have been mostly in my head, and Mom and Grandma certainly had better things to be thinking about.

I couldn't say this to anyone then, but all I wanted was to eat anything tasty that I could get my hands on. This force was so strong I could but yield to it when it grabbed hold of me. If I was playing behind our building or in the playground, the craving drew me back in; if I was in my room, it interrupted what I was doing there and made me go to the kitchen; if I was sitting at the big white table reading, it made me get up and start searching.

And even after I'd eaten what was available, if anything was, it kept tugging at me. It was what was eating me. I'd eaten all the tangerines that first time, yes, I was the one who'd eaten them, but they'd also been eating me. That's what it felt like. Everything that was me disappeared as they ate me, and the taste of them was all that remained.

—

There were times when I saw the plate of pancakes on the counter without my mother first mentioning them to me. Are you going away tonight, I'd ask, and I know I'd once pointed out that she'd promised not to go away anymore. I must have exhausted her so much that she promised the impossible, just to shut me up.

I didn't want the pancakes, but the fact that I would eat them eventually was the only sure thing about the course of the evening. I needed them like I needed the lights in the apartment, and in my head I arranged the rest of my time around this meal. I'd usually sit on the floor and watch children's television programs while I ate; the pancakes would be cold by then and the sugar melted, the liquid had separated from the crystals that crunched like little grains of sand between my teeth, and I ate as slowly as I could so they would last until I started to tire and could go to bed and fall asleep quickly.

I slept in her bed, even when she was at home. As long as that man wasn't there, I got to sleep with her, even after I had long outgrown it, and when I was alone I'd feel a little less scared if I went into her bedroom and lay down and looked at the ceiling and breathed, surrounded by the scent of her in the bedding. I wanted to get tired so I could fall asleep quickly, but under no circumstance could I accidentally fall asleep in front of the television because I knew I'd eventually wake up to the noise that started when the broadcasts were over, which had once scared me so much it couldn't happen again.

—

Sports always seemed to follow the children's programming on television, match reports and news that I didn't understand and only made me feel worse, with their shrill voices and fast talk. I'd get up and switch to the other channel, and one night there was a movie on that I couldn't stop watching even though I knew I shouldn't. There were black-and-white images and a blinding light and several sounds that cut me to the bone. Mothers and children screaming and running on a beach and through a jungle and behind them were billowing pillars of smoke rising like mushrooms into the sky. I heard the terror in the children's cries and saw it in their faces, a horror that drove a spear through my body, and sometimes I still see those black-and-white scenes in my mind, the faces and their contorted expressions, but I don't know where the movie was set or which war it depicted.

My eyes were glued to the screen, the pancake sugar to my mouth. As I watched, I cut thin strips with my knife, and when the plate was empty I sat there because I didn't know what else to do. I started crying, like the children and mothers on the beach. My face contorted too and I thought I had to make myself stop, otherwise I'd cry all night long or until she came home, and I didn't want that. It was weird, because Mom and Grandma had told me I was such a good girl and that's what I wanted to be, I wanted to stop crying, but no matter how hard I tried I couldn't, I just got more scared and the tears just kept coming and I understood that all I could do was ask her to come home. I couldn't stand being on my own.

I'd started school by then. I was big but not big enough. I had to try to get hold of her and make her understand that she had to come home. The invitation to the party she was going to was printed on a yellow balloon she'd shown me because it was funny – imagine being able to send a balloon as a party invitation! – and after that I'd seen it lying on top of the books on a bookshelf in her bedroom. I went in and found it there – there was no phone number on it but I knew what to look for. I sat down on the thick white carpet with the stack of telephone books; next to it was the curling iron she used when getting ready in front of the mirror, and I looked up the name in the directory, but couldn't find it.

I kept flipping through the pages until I realized there was one directory for businesses and another for individuals and when I opened the business directory I found what I was looking for. I dialled the number and let it ring out, rehearsed over and over in my head what I would say when one of her colleagues picked up the phone. But no one answered. I'd gone with her to visit the office where the party was being held, so I could picture their phone in front of me, next to the photocopier on which I'd sometimes make copies of my hands. The phone was the same model as ours but red.

I saw the red phone ringing and ringing, and then I waited and waited until the ringing died out. Then I sat there with the handset in one hand and with the fingers of my other hand I pressed down the plastic cradle it was supposed to be placed on at the end of a call and then I put my index finger in the correct hole in the dial and dialled the number again. Each time, the rings died out and were replaced by a roaring electric buzz that sounded like the end of everything, a sound that was also a silence. I looked at the white telephone jack in the wall and imagined the telephone wires running from our house along the highways into the city and everywhere else. I repeated this several times and then, just as I'd lost hope of anyone answering, the handset was lifted at the other end and a burst of sounds and voices could be heard before it was hung up again. There were people there and she was among them.

—

It was precisely because I'd given up that I'd made contact, I thought. I knew that nothing worked when you wanted it to, but if you thought it wouldn't, it might, and when I tried again I felt renewed hope, expectations I was sure would be dashed again. But this time someone did actually answer. A woman. I told her who I was, my full name, in a firm and confident voice like Mom had taught me, and the woman said something in reply, but there was so much background noise from the party that I couldn't hear and she probably hadn't heard me either when I'd explained that I wanted to talk to my mom.

I repeated myself. I want to talk to my mom, I said again and again, but I couldn't hear what she was saying. There were voices and laughter in the background. A child is on the phone, I heard her say, then there was fresh clamour and the connection was lost. She'd hung up.

After that, I didn't dare call again. I was worked up from those calls and not tired enough to sleep, but at least I'd stopped crying, and in an attempt to distance myself further from what was swelling inside me,

I lay down on the carpet next to the telephone book and began to flip through the thousands of pages. They were thin like in the Bible Mom had been given when she was at school because having one was compulsory. All the numbers that existed, all the surnames and titles and street addresses printed in teeny-tiny letters. I tried to imagine who these names belonged to, approaching the dizzying fact of all these people collected in there. Then I read the pages with the heading 'In Case of War,' which explained what we would do if our country was occupied by a foreign power and that everyone would have to help out more than usual, each at the ready and according to their ability.

But Mom had said that war would never break out here, that this was how people used to think in the old days, so the question was why these pages existed. When I thought about the children running along the beach away from the bombs and all the other children who had to live with war, the tears returned and I couldn't fight them off, no matter how hard I tried. I cried out loud, I cried like a much younger child, and I felt embarrassed even as I was sensing that I almost kind of liked it. I felt sorry for the kids on TV and sorry for myself for being alone. I knew I wouldn't be able to stop crying until I fell asleep or until she came back home, and if she did, I'd have to hurry to dry my tears and try to look normal. If I didn't manage before the front door opened and I heard her out in the hall, I'd turn around and pretend to be asleep so she wouldn't see the state I was in. Spit and snot ran down my chin and cheeks, and my face did not look like itself when I saw myself in the mirror. It was red and swollen and my body felt exhausted, dry inside, as if I had squeezed all the liquid out of it with my tears. I climbed back into bed and laid my head on my mother's pillow, afraid of not being able to fall asleep.

—

I woke with a jolt and shot up in bed, back straight, and looked around the room. It was night and every bulb was still shining, the apartment bathed in lamplight. Everything was as I'd left it, she couldn't have come home. But was she on her way? Something must have woken me up, I thought I'd woken up because she'd come home. Was she in the entrance hall now with her keys in hand, about to slide them into the lock? I listened. Then I turned to see what time it was and how long I'd been asleep. The boxy red numbers on the clock radio on the nightstand by the bed were glowing in the dark as usual, but when I leaned over and saw them, my whole body went cold. They were at 00:00. Time had stopped. No one had said anything to me, I'd never heard of it happening, never seen the numbers like that, but I knew it meant that time had stopped and the world was ending. Everything that allowed the world to exist, all the hours and minutes, had been brought to a standstill and swallowed up by something, and the earth had stopped moving.

I tried to sense it but felt nothing. Maybe the globe was falling freely through infinity. I thought of Grandma and Grandad and wondered if it was happening right now at their place too, or if it had started earlier over there, and if so, what had happened to them? Had they also woken up from it like I had or had they been torn from sleep in their beds by the end of the world and been blown away by it? I didn't dare call them because I remembered what Grandma had sounded like the last time I called when I was home alone – plus Mom had said it wasn't good for me to call Grandma like that. But I had to try to get hold of my mother. Even if she couldn't come home, she had to know what was going on, maybe she already knew, but still I had to call. And if she did know, she'd be on her way home, right?

I slid down to the floor and picked up the phone's big handset and tried again; the phone was grey and when the signals went through, I thought of them in the same hue. I saw them before me like beams of shadow sweeping across ice. I held the handset to my ear and dialled the number again and again. Each time I thought someone at the office in the city would answer, and each time the buzzing tone that began after the ringing ended would finally reach me. If she wasn't here or there – then where was she? I thought about the end, the catastrophe that had begun out there, and imagined it as an avalanche in which everything was falling in a torrent, straight down and into nothingness.

—

Because I'd pulled down the blinds in the bedroom so I wouldn't have to see the darkness through the window, I couldn't see what it looked like outside. I went into the hallway, slowly turned my head, and looked toward the living room window, where the blinds were open. So far nothing, no avalanche and no flames or storms, no glow and no portals to the underworld or the heavens prying open. I went closer to see if I could catch sight of any of what I thought was going on out there, but it was so dark and the light from all the lamps I'd switched on was making the windowpanes even blacker, and my own lurking figure was reflected in them. I jumped high and screamed out loud when I saw it.

I don't know what happened to her that night, but I suppose she was with him. Later, she procured a big white microwave oven for me to heat food in when she wasn't home. She showed me how to use it and started buying Lean Cuisine ready meals that came in clear plastic packages you cut open and poured right onto your plate. They had an almost slimy consistency and an undertaste that came through in every dish, whether it was the bouillabaisse or ratatouille or quiche lorraine that they were meant to resemble.

The microwave oven came with a recipe book describing how to fry slices of bacon on a double layer of paper towels or how to make a kladdkaka chocolate cake in a teacup and omelettes right on the plate. We never ate bacon, nor did we eat kladdkaka. We never actually cooked in the microwave in that way at all. Rather, we used it to defrost Grandma's buns and cookies and heat up those low-calorie ready meals. But the book was there in the kitchen, on top of the microwave, and I'd often leaf through it, reading the recipes and looking at the pictures of the food, more or less fat-free dishes arranged on glossy white porcelain photographed in a way that made everything look like plastic. It was the first cookbook I read regularly after *Now We're Cooking* and the first that I noticed could change the way I was feeling.

In addition to all the usual things I was afraid of, like the dark and hallucinations and Grandma and Grandad dying or Mom not returning home after she went out, I was also afraid of being with other people and of everything that could happen then. The fear made me slow and shut inside myself and encased me like a bell jar much in the same way as my thoughts about food later would. I was afraid of being alone at home and afraid of going out, of the boys who would use their bikes to block the footpath down to the school and the drunks who sat on the bench by the grove, arguing with each other. I was afraid of the bald woman who paced the sidewalk outside, shouting that she was going to murder a famous singer who was often on television at the time, and

I was afraid of the man in the apartment above ours, who'd begun to throw his things out the window.

Mom said he wasn't dangerous, he just wasn't feeling well and didn't know what he was doing. Tools and kitchen utensils and the occasional pair of speakers and a television, all flying like the little birds through the air until they crashed into the rocks on the slope that separated our residential neighbourhood from the road to the factory and industrial zone. You could hear stomping and screaming in the apartment overhead, and I was forever worried that he would come down and plant himself outside our door. She had told me not to answer the door if he rang the bell when I was home alone, and sometimes he'd come down asking to borrow something from us. Then I'd notice that it was difficult for her to get him to leave, she was so polite, and each time I thought he might never leave, because he always seemed to discover that he needed something else or that the first thing he'd asked for wasn't the right thing after all, and he needed to take another look in the toolbox my mother had in the cleaning cabinet in the kitchen.

He never returned what he took, and sometimes I wondered if our things were among those that would end up on the slope. Before I fell asleep at night, I prayed to God to make him disappear, and at last one day he did. His departure gave us a new neighbour, a woman with a little boy. Grandma had said we had to help her because she was on her own, newly arrived from the countryside with no friends or family, it seemed. I think Grandma persuaded Mom to go upstairs and offer to look after the woman's son if needed, or did she do this on her own?

Whatever the case, we started looking after him. The first time it was both me and Mom, but then it fell to me. It was fun being in their home, and I got used to going up there even when they didn't need a babysitter; since she was a teacher they were often home early, and I got to spend as much time with them as I liked when Mom was away and otherwise. I ate dinner with them whenever she offered and I was given my own key so I could let myself in even when they weren't home.

Their kitchen had the same sink and rows of cabinets and the same eating area in front of the window, exactly the same as ours but brighter because it was on the first floor, and from there you could almost see the entire playground, which she thought was so good, it would be so good when her son grew up because she was on her own with him, she said. Otherwise she never said anything about it, just like my mother never said anything about being on her own with me and why that was, nothing beyond that she didn't want us to live in another country, like my father. Our building and the rows of buildings on our street were full of mothers on their own with their children, and just as I never asked my mother anything else about my father, I never asked why the father of this woman's child was elsewhere.

—

It smelled of lentils and brown rice up there and she'd be peeling carrots and cutting them up for us while she cooked dinner, often a thick sauce with eggplant and zucchini and mushrooms that all three of us liked, with onions and crème fraîche, which was a new thing in the stores that all the mothers had started to use. It could be tasty, but sometimes it made the food sour and gritty. She taught me how to make root vegetable hash and potato soup with leeks, and sometimes she made toasted sandwiches in a special sandwich iron and showed me that you could add a banana to them, banana and cheese and tomato paste or banana and Falun sausage and curry. I wrote down all of her recipes in pencil on lined paper, which I put in a folder and tucked in between the pages of *Now We're Cooking*.

One day she rang our doorbell and asked me to come up. She had little pimples on her face, which she apologized for as soon as I came in, before I even noticed them. I probably wouldn't have if she hadn't said anything. In the kitchen, her little son was sitting in his high chair, and in the middle of the kitchen table were two large chocolate bars she'd bought, one with nuts and one pure milk chocolate, and next to them two packages of English graham crackers, one roll of orange chocolate pieces, and another roll of toffee-filled. The bag from the grocery store was on the floor under the table, I saw. She asked me to sit down and brought out a pot of hot chocolate she'd made. Real hot chocolate, she said with a smile, like the one I got at my mom and dad's house and into which I dipped sandwiches made of sweetened bread when I was your age.

She'd never mentioned her parents before. It sounded so strange to hear her talk about them, and I couldn't imagine her having been a child like me. I talked to her son and fastened his bib while she poured the steaming chocolate into our two large teacups and his plastic children's cup. Then she sat down across from me and started tearing the wrappers off the chocolate. I watched her pour the rolls into small bowls and break the solid chocolate bars into squares and place them on two plates. Her hands moved quickly and habitually, as if this was a ritual.

She stood up again and brought us small spoons and showed us how to put one piece of chocolate at a time on the spoon and dip it in the hot chocolate until it started to melt and become soft, and then put it between two graham crackers. You haven't gotten your period yet, have you? she asked me, and I shook my head, I was only ten or eleven, and she said her period was about to start and this was the only thing that eased the way it made her feel, chocolate was the only thing that could make it better, she said. My teeth hurt as I bit into the two graham crackers sandwiching a sticky piece of chocolate, and I ran my tongue over my teeth as if that would relieve the pain.

My teeth were uneven and rough from all the fillings. The fact that they were weak had been discovered during my first visit to the dentist, where it turned out I had thirteen cavities. I was given an anesthetic but couldn't stop myself from screaming and crying, and it felt like a punishment to have to go back several times. I hated my teeth and I hated my mom for letting me get all those cavities. She said it was because I used to fall asleep with the bottle in my mouth, and I was so full of rage I thought I might explode. But what she said must have been true, that she hadn't been able to wake me up, because I think I can remember what it was like to be that young and drink the milky gruel. The thick, sickly sweet liquid that gushed out when I pressed the nipple against my palate with my tongue, the warmth and the rhythm and how I seemed to drift away with it.

When I started looking after the neighbour boy, I often warmed gruel for him in the evenings and I loved to lie beside him and watch him hold the bottle and drain it. He'd lie close to me while drinking, his eyes half shut, mouth moving as if of its own accord, and after half the bottle he'd no longer be looking at me but staring into nothing.

Even after he stopped drinking gruel, I thought he smelled of it and you could still smell it throughout their apartment. I liked being there because it made me feel like I had a purpose, like I was needed in their home.

His mother often said she enjoyed talking to me and I remember liking her and her wanting my help. Even though I was only a child, it felt as if my presence made things easier somehow or made her less lonely. And maybe I'd filled a special function when she asked me to come upstairs that day. Maybe she wanted me there so it wouldn't feel quite so inappropriate to eat in the way she had planned. Had she? Had she planned on gorging herself with him beside her at the table but had changed her mind and so went downstairs to fetch me? Or was she just going to eat a little and leave the rest be? Maybe she wasn't like me at all, but one of those people who could – who could eat a little and leave the rest. As many say they do. It was the reasonable course of action – reasonable for her to do this when her declining estrogen and serotonin levels demanded it, and that's all there was to it, anything else is no more than a thought she never had that has only taken shape in me.

—

I seem to remember things revolving around food in their home too, but maybe it was only me who was constantly thinking about eating and where I might find a tasty morsel. She would whip up rosehip soup that we ate cold or hot in the afternoons, with vanilla ice cream and tiny almond biscuits, and in the evening after dinner, when I'd read a story to her son and she had corrected her students' papers, she'd take out a bowl of chocolate, even though it was a normal weekday, or stand up and bake a special caramel tart with lingonberries or pears, for which I was also given the recipe.

Mom said she should give her money because I ate there so often, but I don't know if she ever did. I don't know if she thought about how much I ate. As for me, I'd probably already realized that my hunger would not be stilled, no matter how much I put in my mouth. I wanted to fill myself up until there was no room for anything else, and I thought that food bound me to the world, like a true sign that I belonged to it. And that I was not devil spawn but a human being like everyone else, the kind who made their way through life so easily, without being afraid or forever occupied by thoughts about everything.

The third cookbook I read was *Mastering the Art of French Cooking*, which I took down from the shelf in the kitchen one Saturday while my mother was working in her room as usual and I had nothing to do and couldn't find anything else I wanted to read. I'd already flipped through most of the books she had that intrigued me, mostly novels by female authors who looked so mysterious and beautiful in their author photos on the flaps of the dust jacket. *Mastering the Art of French Cooking* was a thick paperback with a pattern of French lilies on the front cover and thin yellowed pages, and it promised to equip a person with all the essential cooking skills, divided into ten chapters.

My favourite passage began with an instruction to go outside and chop down a small juniper tree and build a fire in your wood stove, then grill or maybe smoke something over it. For years I've carried the memory of that part of the book as well as reading it while sitting at the big white table, and I've often wondered what sort of recipe it might have been, but looking through the book now I see there is no such entry. There were many old cookbooks in our home; I must have read this in a different one and confused the two in my memory. Or maybe I created that image all on my own, maybe there's no recipe in the world with those instructions. But the nineteen-page section on soufflés is there in any case. I loved reading it and imagining the mixed batter, the aroma unfurling, and the soufflé magically rising in the oven, and that you had to make sure all the windows were shut before you took it out.

The book had sat on the shelf above the extractor fan over our stove and was previously in the kitchen in the apartment my mother shared with my father before I was born, in a different city. In it she had learned how to whisk fluffy mayonnaise for his lobsters and langoustines and to finely chop shallots for the pinkish mignonette sauce that was to be on the table when there were oysters for dinner. I knew that oysters were special because they were at their best during certain months of the year – in the summer they were fatty and milky – and I soon realized that all food that was special was special because it wasn't available year-round or wasn't as good out of season. You had to wait for it. Oysters and lobsters had their special time, as did the white asparagus and mushrooms and primeurs that my mother and her friends longed for, as did the blackberries that grew in the rocky crevices of the island where my paternal grandfather's house and my father's old cottage were.

—

When I wasn't at Grandma and Grandad's during school holidays, that's where Mom and I went. In the years before I was born, she and my father had fished for lobster in those waters, setting nets to catch plaice and cod, and diving for oysters in a spot where you could pick three hundred in an hour. Later, when we were there without him, she still took the boat out to go fishing with a girlfriend of hers. One time they caught a lobster that weighed more than three and a half kilograms; they tossed it into a blue milk crate on the cabin sole, and my mother's friend shouted to me through the wind: Don't you touch that! The lobster looked like a monster or a primordial creature as it crawled around in the bin, swiping and snapping its claws in the air. I pressed myself against the rail and looked the other way, out over the grey sea, the lashing rain, toward the lighthouse and the narrows opening onto the distant horizon. I'd come to hear those words repeated so often. Don't you touch that! The memory of that scene would make the adults laugh out loud, and as I grew older I got the joke: no small child would voluntarily touch a large live lobster.

—

The sauce chapter in *Mastering the Art of French Cooking* was even more well-thumbed than the others, the crumpled and folded pages with little splashes here and there that made me wonder. I understood that my mother's life with my father was different from the one she and I lived, and each time she told me about it, a longing was awakened in me. She'd watched him grab hold of his lobsters on the kitchen counter and take a big knife and split them alive and put them in a big steaming cast-iron pan with a lot of butter and heads of dill – but when such preparations fell to her, she didn't dare drive the knife into the live lobster; instead she'd toss it straight into a big pot of boiling water. We'd eat them boiled like that, as they were, or with butter that she clarified in a milk pan, into which she might crush some garlic, if there was any, and she said she was going to learn how to hold them still long enough to cut through the head with the tip of the knife and split them, but I never saw her do it.

If it was too windy, I had to stay home when they took the boat out to drag up their creels and nets. One time I was down on the beach picking up starfish and moon jellyfish the currents had washed up on the sand overnight. I was planning on throwing them back into the sea so they could continue their lives down there, lives we knew so little about, but first I would carry them to the house and show them to my mother. I'd just seen her sail in from the strait and enter the bay with the boathouses.

I made my way barefoot, bucket in hand, up the little paved walkway leading away from the shore. Walking carefully so not too much sea water would splash out, I passed the sundial and the glass table and the old garden furniture with faded plastic straps that dug into my thighs and buttocks when I sat on them without my clothes. When I got to the house and walked into the kitchen with the bucket, they were already there. I got that feeling I'd get from being close to her again after she'd been gone, or knowing I was, even if she was out of sight. Water was boiling in the biggest pots on the stove and on the kitchen floor was the milk crate with something shiny and black inside. The second I took a closer look, there was movement and the two lobsters that had been on top, atop the others, slipped out and onto the floor. There they crawled around, their claws scraping the stone slabs and their antennae slowly waving in the air. Their little peppercorn eyes stared at me and I hastily backed out the kitchen door, tripped on the stairs, and lost my grip on the bucket containing the starfish and jellyfish.

The bucket fell out of my hand and rolled away. I shouted for my mother and she came and picked me up. She was there. I was afraid she would see that I'd dropped the bucket, but she just carried me straight into the kitchen, and when she saw the lobsters on the floor she swore out loud and stood me on a chair and told me to stay put. I stayed still and watched as she picked them up and pressed them one by one into the pots. I stared at the boiling water and thought about how they'd go still and die in there, like drowning in the old days when fishermen couldn't swim. She hugged me and lifted me off the chair, then she fished the wet sea creatures out of their pots with a pair of large tongs and placed them on a platter she'd already set on the table. The sight of their brilliant colour calmed me when I sat down at the table. No doubt about it, they were good and dead.

—

The adults ate two each and as they ate they talked about the nets and the creels and the sea outside and the people who lived on the other islands. I ate bread and a tail and a claw that I helped myself to and managed to get the meat out whole from the shell after my mother cracked it open for me, her long freckled fingers gripping the claw, then a quick squeeze of the tool that looked like the nutcracker Grandma took out at Christmas. I tasted the mayonnaise and couldn't understand why anyone would want to eat something like that; I felt full and sleepy because of the food and the wind whining against the windows, but I kept myself awake so I could keep listening to the adults.

When we were there, I loved doing that. Otherwise not, I mostly wanted to shut up the people who I heard talking at home in our apartment when there was a party and when I got to go along to the pub, but in the house on the island, in the room referred to as the salon even though it was a small room, the conversations sounded completely different. They seemed harmless and happy. I waited for the giggles and the guffaws and liked the way they so often recounted the same stories when we sat there, like the one about the windy autumn when they set their nets and caught so many plaice that they had plaice and red wine for dinner every night until the wine ran out and they had to order more from the mainland. There had been two days of storm, and they had to make do without wine, but on the third day they could finally go and collect their box from the delivery point. The rain was pouring down as they lugged that cardboard box and it got so wet that they were afraid the bottom would give out and the wine bottles would end up shattered on the hill on their way down to the harbour, but they managed it and got into the boat and put a tarp over the box, only to get out to the island and up to the house and find that it contained no plonk, as they called it, but Parfait d'Amour, Eau-de-Vie, and banana liqueur, several bottles of each. They laughed so hard they'd be screaming when they got to the part where the delivery point called to say that a sailor had come in who was angry because he'd ordered three different kinds of digestifs and got a lot of cheap red wine instead, and I'd be laughing too, because they were laughing and because I liked the words they were saying so very much: Parfait d'Amour, Eau-de-Vie, banana liqueur.

I don't know if it was that story or something else they were recalling, but I forgot all about my bucket and the starfish and the little moon jellies, the names I was going to give them and all my thoughts about how I was going to keep them, and I didn't think of them again until the following day. When I got up and came into the salon, it smelled like it usually did in the early morning – cigarette smoke blended with the damp sea air that would find its way in with the wind, even if the door and all the windows were shut – and when I went out on the steps to retrieve them, I saw that they'd dried on the ground.

—

The island was full of traces of my father. It was his island even more than Mom's and mine, and the man she was with never joined us there, not once. I didn't know what the man who was my father was doing or why he'd moved so far away and why my mom hadn't wanted us to live with him there. I never knew when or if he would get in touch, and it didn't happen often enough for me to get used to it.

Even though I thought about him often, it was a surprise each time he reached out. I didn't know what to say to him and what I knew of him, what I knew about where he came from and what I gleaned from the postcards he sent from his travels, and the gifts that my mother and all the other adults looked at and touched with such wonder and careful observation made me think he must be very rich and important and special, and I could never be the kind of child he'd want to have. I was afraid he would call in hopes of talking to me and I would be made to talk to him; at the same time, it's what I wanted.

—

When I was old enough to travel on my own, I was afraid of being sent to visit him, in that other country where he lived or in the new summer place he'd acquired. The first time I visited it, he'd picked wild strawberries and threaded them onto a blade of grass for me. He was holding it when I arrived and handed it to me. I recognized him, but he was shorter and thinner than I'd remembered.

It seemed strange that this man who took up so much space in my imagination would be so small in reality. He called his new place a cottage, just like the cottage on the island, but it was bigger than the whole apartment where I lived with my mom, and was situated high above a narrow bay where his boats were moored and had large windows that looked out on them and the archipelago across the bay.

I had eaten breakfast and my mother had added a piece of fruit to my packed lunch that day, still I was very hungry when I arrived. It was afternoon – he took my bag, hugged me, and led the way over some rocks and up the steps that went over the hill to the house. He said he'd bought it two years earlier and I wondered why he hadn't invited me to come until now, but I didn't ask. When we got inside, he took me to the guest room opposite his bedroom and put my backpack on the floor in front of the bed. The backpack was from a particular brand, which was too pricey really but which I had coveted for a long time and finally was given. It was very nice, but inside that linseed-scented room with curtains in classic floral patterns and a bed built into the wall with grooved and beaded panels painted light grey, it looked so plasticky and dumb.

He showed me the bathroom where I was to wash my hands, as well as the rest of the house, which was made up of one big room with an open-plan kitchen at one end. Open shelving, copper pots, clay vessels, big knives. There was a wood-burning stove and a shiny steel AGA with many burners and several ovens, but no microwave and no other appliances as far as I could see, except for a small shiny silver machine with a long lever and a water kettle with a bird on the spout. He told me he'd grilled my mother about my eating habits, showed me a dish filled with even more wild strawberries that he had picked behind the house that morning, and white packages containing cod loins in the fridge.

Are you hungry? he asked, and I tried to nod a little but didn't dare say yes. I could never admit that I was hungry, not to anyone but Mom and Grandma, nor that I was tired or had a pain somewhere or was angry or sad or worried either. I'd deny it if someone asked, or not say anything. He pulled out a packet of graham crackers and I thought he was going to give me one to eat, but instead he asked me to crush them and put them in a pie tin on the counter. It was for the dessert, he called it cheesecake. Mom had told him I didn't like cream and neither did he, he said, and took out gelatin leaves that he soaked in a bowl of water. I watched everything he did; he moved so elegantly and carefully among the work surfaces and tools. This wasn't quite how I'd imagined him.

To make sure I could follow his instructions to the letter, I kept myself on edge. Everything I did had to be just right, I thought. I had to mix the batter for the cheesecake and help spread it over the graham cracker crumbs, and while it was in the oven we'd have a drink. He brought out a small bowl of chips and then he poured orange juice for me, and for himself white wine so cold it fogged up his glass. When we sat down, he said cheers and welcome, then took a small sip and looked me in the eye as he swallowed and I did the same. The juice was somehow thicker and had a much stronger flavour than the frozen juice we sometimes had at home. He asked me how things were with my mom, how I was doing at school and what grade I was in now, what subjects I liked and if I had friends. I had to search for the words and I thought I was finding them at a decent pace, but when he stopped asking questions, I didn't know if I should say anything else, and if so, what.

He sat in silence and I sat in silence. It felt like an occasion to be there with him in that big room, but I didn't really know if I was embarrassed or happy and I didn't know what to say to him and how my voice would sound if I opened my mouth before I knew exactly which words it would produce. He pointed to the small bowl that stood between us on the low pale wood table by the fireplace and asked if I didn't like potato chips, and I lied and said yes actually I did and reached for them across the table.

My dad's potato chips were nothing like the ones I'd tasted before. I had a friend whose dad used to come home with potato chips and burgers on Fridays. He was self-employed, which was unusual, he loved McDonald's and all the other American fast food that I never ate with my mother, and it was as if the greasy paper bags of hamburgers and pop and fries that he brought home and set out on the coffee table in their television room represented something he had elevated in his mind and wanted to turn into a shared aspiration for the family.

I usually went home when they were about to start eating their hamburgers. Once I was asked to stay for the meal because one of the older sons hadn't come home in time, but I couldn't finish the hamburger they gave me because the sauce on it tasted of something spoiled and metallic, and the potato chips, which they'd piled into a big plastic bowl, had an impossible synthetic smell that spread through the room as soon as their package was opened, making it difficult to breathe. They went floury and soft in the mouth, but the ones my dad had poured into the little bowl on the table between us by the fireplace were different, crisp and crunchy, smelling only of salt and a hint of oil. After I finished the first one, I helped myself to another, and while I nibbled at it, I looked at the paintings and furniture in the room, the water beyond the windows. Everything was so beautiful and I wondered why we didn't have a house like this and why I didn't live with him.

———

I had to pee and held it for a long time before I dared get up and say that I needed the toilet. It was as if I had lost the ability to move; I couldn't say anything or get out of the chair and therefore waited until the very last second. When I was done and sat back down, my father sipped his wine and I sipped my juice and then he made his way to the stove, where he put on a big pot of new potatoes he'd bought earlier in the day. He'd taken the boat to another island and had also picked chanterelles, which he fried in butter that he made froth and sizzle before adding them and then he took out bread and sliced it and fried little sandwiches he said would be our appetizer. He kept inviting me to help or to watch when he did something tricky. I watched his hands and how he worked with them in a way that I'd probably never seen anyone do before, calm and methodical and with small, considered movements.

I'd never imagined him like this. My many fantasies about him had never been about cooking. If I had imagined him cooking, it would have been as I imagined a man, someone who quickly threw something together in the kitchen, and preferred going out to eat at a restaurant or letting someone else cook. That's how I imagined him. I couldn't square this with the reality of him cooking and doing it with such careful precision. As he went along, he commented on everything he did and why. He shared his special trick to get a perfectly boiled egg and he explained everything step by step, how he first boiled water in a kettle, put the eggs in a pan with a lot of salt, and poured the boiling water over them. Then they'd boil for seven minutes, eight if they'd been in the fridge, but eggs shouldn't be stored like that because most recipes required them to be room temperature. And if they cracked during the vigorous boil, the salt would prevent the egg white from seeping out.

He whipped up a glossy béchamel sauce that smelled of warm milk, and when the eggs were done, I had to rinse them in cold water, peel them, and chop them for the sauce. He showed me how to hold the egg under the stream of water to get all the shell off as I carefully removed it from the soft whites with help of the membrane in between, and I tried to cut my eggs into pieces of about the same size and get them all into the saucepan.

Perfect, he said, looking at me. Very nicely diced.

Then he asked me to set the table. I looked around and tried to figure out which china to use. When he handed it to me, I moved as slowly and carefully as I could, setting the plates down softly on the long oak table and putting the cutlery down in the same way. I'm sorry, I forgot these, he said, handing me two folded kitchen towels woven in a checkered pattern. I didn't know what to do with them, so I held on to them and stood by the table and thought about it for a long time, until I saw the embroidered monogram and remembered a book Grandma had given me about a girl who worked for a family where they used cloth napkins with initials on them, which she had to wash and iron after each use.

I put the napkins under the silverware next to our plates, as straight as I could. He stayed by the stove, steaming the cod loins and pouring some of the liquid from the pan into the sauce, snipping the dill over it and stirring. I looked at his body, which was the origin of my own, perhaps more so than my mother's, I thought, since it was from him that the first seed came – and when everything was ready we ate together at the long table; I counted eight chairs on each side. He poured ice water with a slice of lemon into a tall wineglass for me, and I spent some more time looking at all the objects and works of art. I'd always liked my home and Mother's and everything in it, but now I was struck by how simple it was in comparison, so ugly and claustrophobic, and its location was bland and banal. No nature except for some trees in a boring grove, no water except for the rain puddles and a lake so small you could walk around it in less than an hour.

~

I'd been worried that I wouldn't be able to finish what he put on my plate, but the portion was just right and everything tasted so good. It was easy and fun to eat. He praised the egg sauce as if I had made it, I told him that cod with egg sauce was my favourite dish, he nodded and smiled, and I felt stupid when I realized he must have known. Mom must have told him. It was strange to think they'd talked to each other about me.

He cleared the table and told me to come to the kitchen counter and put the wild strawberries on the cheesecake. It looked like a cake, which made me nervous since I couldn't eat cake and there was no one to whom I could smuggle my slice. That's what I did at every birthday party where cake was served, and if that didn't work, I had to sit there pushing my spoon around in the cream to make it look like I'd at least eaten a little, but when I took a small bite I realized that cheesecake was not the same. It was light and soft and its flavour was not nauseating at all, but fresh and tasty.

By the time we finished eating, it had started to get dark outside. The water looked bluish black. He suggested we move to the armchairs by the fireplace again. He put a new log on the fire and let me light a few candles and then he started that shiny machine, which turned out would make coffee if you placed a small cup in it; it filled the whole room with its aroma, and when the coffee was ready he got a bottle and poured something dark in a small glass for himself and took out his cigarillos. One cigarette after dinner is fine, he said, looking at me. But no more than that, I nodded and for a moment I thought he was going to give me one.

Thinking about it now, I wonder if he really did stick to smoking just one. Was he the type who could? The smoke smelled faintly of tar and there was something about everything we'd eaten and how we were sitting there together that made me feel grown-up, but then I got tired and was reminded that I wasn't. I looked into the fire burning in the fireplace and nodded as he spoke. I looked at the glowing logs and the flames licking them, but after a while I couldn't focus my gaze. My eyelids kept shutting, no matter how hard I tried to keep them open. I wanted to be awake and sit there with him for a long time, but I was so sleepy, and at my temples was a dull ache that felt grey and prickly and slowly filled my head with pressure from within.

The next time I saw him it was in the city where he lived and he'd made spaghetti with meat sauce. A classic bolognese, in his words. Well, his wife might have been the one to make it of course, but I've always assumed it was him, because he liked to cook and because that kind of dish benefits from being prepared in advance and left to stand for a while as you get on with other things.

I was older then and I don't know if he'd asked my mother what I liked or if he thought I should be able to eat most things. Pasta bolognese was a meat dish considered universally liked by children and one I could eat and liked because it didn't really taste like meat.

I remember my mother making it once when my friend from the community garden village spent the weekend at our place. What child doesn't like spaghetti and meat sauce? she hissed as she stood in the kitchen afterwards, scraping my friend's plate clean. I told her I was sure he liked it, but he was probably used to the meat sauce his mother made, without the added garlic and wine and cayenne pepper and nutmeg, and my mother laughed loudly and with a measure of triumph, as if she wanted her laughter to communicate that she should have guessed as much, it was so typical of the people who lived down there not to spice their food. I liked my mother's meat sauce very much, but I didn't tell her that I also liked the other version, the sweet, shiny kind my friend's mother would make, the pile of pale spaghetti, thick and overcooked, limp on the plate.

⁓

As soon as I woke up that morning I could tell I wasn't feeling well. I was in middle school and this was during summer vacation; my mother and her boyfriend were going to spend the summer in the city where my father lived and I was joining them for a spell, in a narrow house with several floors and many stairs. I'd never had a headache like this before, it was pressing against my temples, billowing like thick smoke in my skull. I thought I might faint as I walked down the stairs in that house, and I remember my mother looking at me and asking how I was doing when we saw each other in the hallway outside the kitchen on the ground floor, but I told her it was nothing, because I thought the pain might go away if I ignored it.

As I did every other morning there, I went out for breakfast at a hamburger restaurant down the street. There was never anything I wanted in the fridge, and my mother and her boyfriend hardly ate either. They spent their mornings in the bedroom on the top floor. It had its own bathroom and a roof terrace with Mediterranean plants in big pots and wrought-iron garden furniture, and it was as if that top floor swallowed them up. Like when he was at our house, they shut themselves away, they might go to bed early or sleep all day, but at home I could see when her bedroom door was closed. Of course here I couldn't see the top floor if I was sitting in the kitchen or the living room downstairs after they'd gone up, and so their absence was even more like disappearing, similar to how I felt myself disappearing sometimes.

It felt as if I were all alone in that unfamiliar house with wall-to-wall carpeting, the smell of cleaning products and something rotting on the lower level, and the whole great unknown city outside. Sometimes there were crackers or cookies in one of the kitchen cupboards and on the counter would usually be money that might have been meant for me and I'd take it and go out in the mornings. I couldn't be in the house while they were sleeping or whatever.

The front door put you right on the street, and outside everyone else's door stood glass bottles full of milk. I liked seeing the milk bottles and I liked the way the air felt outside the row of small white plaster and brown brick terraced houses with their black cast-iron fences along the sidewalks.

—

I hadn't yet learned to like hamburgers back then; even so I visited the Wimpy's every morning at the big intersection a short distance from the house. Of course, I could have gone to any of the cafés in the area, but I probably didn't dare enter any of them because it wasn't quite clear to me how things were done, whether you should go in and take a seat at a table and wait for someone to take your order or go straight to the cash register and place your order and pay right away. I think I tried – it was likely that I tried to muster the courage every morning but would invariably end up at Wimpy's.

There I didn't have to worry that my money wouldn't stretch. I could order from the bright breakfast menu above the cash registers and see exactly what everything cost, a toasted egg-and-cheese muffin and a hot chocolate, and I got the tray and sat down in a solitary spot by the window looking out over the wide street lined with tall trees while I ate and drank the hot chocolate, which was watery but incredibly sweet.

I don't remember how that day unfolded, but I remember being afraid of what it would be like to see him again. In the early evening, my mother brought me to the place in the middle of the city, near my father's office, where they'd agreed we'd meet. I looked on as they gave each other a quick hug and saw his eyes when he looked at her, as if he were instantly consumed by thoughts about something that related only to them, and then she hugged me and said goodbye and vanished among the rush of people around there. Well, he said, shall we be off? Instead of using my proper name, he kept using the nickname I'd had when I was little, the one no one called me anymore. He wrote it on all the letters and cards he sent me too. Maybe he didn't know that I was in fact called something else now, I thought. He looked at me with that little smile in the corner of his mouth that, like his voice, was one of the things about him I'd started to recognize, that I knew exactly what they were like and would never forget.

He wore a grey suit, tie, and white shirt and had draped his coat over one arm because it was hot outside. I didn't know you'd gone punk, he said, and I looked down at my shoes and the trousers I'd sewn myself, feeling self-conscious and thinking that true punks would cringe at him saying that. Are you hungry? he asked. No, I said. That wasn't true, I hadn't eaten since breakfast, but I didn't seem able to say as much. I couldn't utter the word *yes*, couldn't say his assumption was correct, I did need to eat. Right, good, he said.

Being with him was unreal. I didn't dare look straight at him but kept trying to glance furtively at him to take in every aspect of his appearance and the movements he made. He said we were going to buy me a book and we went into one of the quieter streets and came to a bookshop where it was crowded and hot and full of books from floor to ceiling. He walked up to the information desk to retrieve the book he'd put aside for me. The way he looked at me as we stood together in the line for the cashier made me feel like we belonged together, yet clearly we didn't because I didn't know him even though we were as close as two people could be; he was my dad who I knew nothing about. There was something about being with him in his city, talking to each other in our language while everyone around us spoke another, that made it seem like we shared an invisible bond.

The book was given to me in a thin paper bag, a collection of poems about cats, and the musical we were going to see was also about cats. I wondered if we were going to eat something, after all, and if I'd find a way to tell him I'd worked up a small appetite nonetheless. It was hard to follow what was happening between the singing cats onstage. I couldn't wait for it to end, but I wanted nothing more than to sit like that, beside him in silence in the dark theatre, smelling his scent and wondering who he was. What he looked like when he moved through the city on his own, when he was at work, when he was with his wife.

I knew nothing.

But I was really hungry and I felt like I was going to faint in the chair, my head was so sore and as if numbed by the pain that had pushed its way in and cast itself over everything else. We hadn't eaten and I hadn't dared to ask if we were going to either, but when the show was over he explained that we were going to take a car to his house, and when we got there and walked from the street through the front door, the meat sauce was waiting on the stove in the kitchen and I smelled it right away.

I'd never been in a house like his before and it was unlike anything I'd ever seen, inside or out. I didn't know what to say and couldn't concentrate on what my father and his wife were saying to me because there was so much I wanted to look at. I tried to take it all in without looking like I was staring. Before dinner we were to have a drink. I chose orange juice and it was almost even thicker and tastier than the one I'd had at his summer place. They drank something with alcohol in it and then we moved into the kitchen, which was large and looked old-fashioned although everything seemed new, and the man who was my father took his place by the stove and boiled pasta while his wife showed me to my chair.

The dining table was long, with baluster legs, and looked like it was meant to be next to an olive grove somewhere in a warmer country. He brought out a grater, a large cheese he said was called pecorino, and a round wooden board with the word BREAD carved into it; there had been three almost identical boards in a pile, and I remember thinking they looked so nice stacked on top of each other on the wide kitchen counter, which was made of marble and inset with a white porcelain sink with copper taps.

They had a large wine fridge in the kitchen, and he took out a bottle and uncorked it and set it out. I'd been so eager to eat, but by the time we were sitting at that beautiful table, I wasn't hungry anymore and could hardly talk because my head had started to hurt again and it hurt so much I felt paralyzed and cut off from everything else. Fortunately, neither of them seemed to notice that anything was the matter with me. As soon as I'd sat down, I remembered to put the napkin in my lap before doing anything else. I looked at the big bottle of Italian mineral water in front of me, the label with the red star, and my father's wife filled my glass, and with a delicate hand I raised it to my mouth to drink. My father served me a large ladle of the tagliatelle, fresh from the stove, spooned hot bolognese on top, and picked up the pecorino and grated it over my plate.

If I invoke the smells of that kitchen, it makes me think this was probably a very good bolognese, with pancetta and chicken hearts browned in olive oil, and onions, but at the time I could barely taste it because I was so focused on sitting up straight and speaking properly and figuring out what to say to my father and his wife. Garlic should never be in a bolognese, he said, and it should be milk, not cream. And white wine. I must remember to tell my mother, I thought, because she used red wine and garlic, and perhaps the other mothers had been more correct, those whose meat sauces she'd laughed at, with milk and no garlic.

I made sure to catch only a few tagliatelle at a time, so the bite wouldn't be too big after I spun them on my fork. I ate as carefully as I could so as not to spill or get food around my mouth. Periodically I would pick up the napkin and wipe my lips with a corner of it, and every now and then I set my cutlery on the plate and rested my hands in my lap.

I ate slowly, but it wasn't just to make the food last as long as possible, it was also to try to tame my hunger by taking small, small bites and make myself smaller. I'd inherited my paternal grandfather's broad jawline and my maternal grandfather's big bones; these men's bodies lived on in me, as well as my mother's duck-like feet and Grandma's sausage fingers. I was tall and broad-shouldered, and when I ate I often felt like I was growing and getting even bigger. My mother would tell me I needed to be braver and take up more space, but I didn't want to take up any space at all, especially with my body. I wanted to be small and dainty like she had been as a child and like my dad's wife was too, slim and elegant just like him.

I had also learned that this was how you were supposed to eat because it was good for the digestion and more pleasurable and made it easier to converse with the others at the table. And even though there was usually no one else around when I ate, it's what I was wishing for, but now that I was sitting there with my father and his wife, I didn't know what to say to them. She asked me questions about ordinary things that shouldn't have been so difficult to talk about, but I wouldn't even have known how to respond in my own language, and finding the right words seemed impossible. They came in spurts, a few sentences at a time, and I had to keep searching for new ones.

I sat with my arms at my sides, trying to look awake and alert. Whenever I wanted adults to think I was lovely, I tried to arrange my face like that, aware I had a tendency to look lethargic and absent, and in that moment I most certainly did. It felt as if my face had gone numb and was hanging like a heavy porridge. I was so tired I could have fallen asleep right there at the table. I'd waited so long for this, but now that I was finally in it, it was like I wasn't really there.

I didn't dare look at my father's wife and instead kept my eyes on my plate, where the sauce coated the ribbons of pasta wrapping around each other. I searched the tagliatelle and everywhere inside me for something to say, but it was as if I suddenly knew nothing about myself or anything else she was asking about, and couldn't relate anything.

Then I heard her say that she thought I could speak well and then I remembered what I'd wanted to tell her, but in the middle of the sentence I was managing to get out, it was as if I could no longer see, my vision blurred and everything around me slipped away, their faces and the wine-glasses and the food. I blacked out and must have fallen or slipped off my chair, because the next moment I was very close to the checkered stone floor and could feel something warm and wet coming out of my mouth.

I projectile vomited, and when I could see again I saw the spew of chewed-up tagliatelle splattered on the baluster legs and flowing over the limestone floor tiles. It was unbelievable. I didn't understand how it could have happened – me, vomiting. I heard them talking somewhere far away and I noticed myself being pulled off the floor and set back on the chair and one of them gave me water. His wife told my father that if I wasn't feeling well I'd probably want to go home to my mother and I heard them place a call.

I can no longer remember if he went with me or if I was alone in the car that took me back to my mother and her boyfriend. My dad had called to tell her I'd vomited; again it felt so strange to know they'd spoken to each other, and I was ashamed of the reason why: my unpredictable body. The whole day leading up to our meeting I'd been anxious, and yet I'd never imagined a thing like this could happen.

—

It was the last time I saw him that summer, even though my mother and I stayed in that city for a while. He was going away himself, and then it was time for me to go home, or to Grandma and Grandad rather, so that my mother and the man she for some reason wanted to be with so badly could go on the vacation they'd planned. Only years later did I realize that the poems in T. S. Eliot's *Old Possum's Book of Practical Cats* were the basis for the musical, and my father had planned it so that we'd go see *Cats*, like everyone else, except I'd get the collection of poems too. Maybe my mother had told him that I liked to read or maybe he'd just thought it was a good way to go about it.

It didn't really matter what the books I read as a child were about, the important thing was how they made me feel, I needed to feel like I couldn't put them down. I wanted to be so absorbed in reading that I forgot everything else. I read anything that could grab me in that way, non-fiction about colonialism and archaeology, the old 'girls' stories' that someone gave us a whole box of, encyclopedias, picture books about children in other countries and chapter books and my mother's novels.

I often read about young women in the past, working in inhuman conditions, for families and on estates and farms. In the women's association book clubs my grandmother was involved in, they often chose books like that. It boggles the mind now, Grandma would say when she'd show them to me, but that's exactly how it was. Usually she was laconic, saying no more than I had to read this or that book when I grew up, and I'd understand that it was something singular, especially when she couldn't or wouldn't explain what was so good about it.

Her reading was the only other thing that was almost as exclusive as her eating, the way she slipped away eating a peach or a freshly baked cinnamon bun while handing me one. Everything else she did involved the rest of us. Everything else could be interrupted at any time by anyone and seemed to keep her perpetually open and available to us.

At first I'd mostly flipped through the cookbooks, for lack of anything else or because they happened to be lying around, at home or at Grandma and Grandad's, but I noticed that reading cookbooks, or parts of them anyway, was like residing in the sections of other books that dealt with food: the Famous Five books where the children ate potted meat and jam sandwiches after they'd been on one of their adventures in caves and haunted castles, or *Winnie-the-Pooh* when Pooh and Christopher Robin packed a lunch bag for an outing, or at the beginning of the first Paddington book where Mrs. Brown brought Paddington along to a bakery after he ate the marmalade sandwich he'd been carrying under his hat.

In the autobiography of one of my favourite authors, I read about how they ate at the boarding school he attended as a child. I was interested in such things because had my mother not left my father, she said, I'd probably have gone to boarding school. That stuck with me, and there was also something familiar about the handling of all things edible at those schools; I read about how the students in the dormitories secreted away biscuits and sweets and fruit that their parents sent them – familiar because I wanted my own hidden stash too, when I was at home with my mother but especially when I had to travel to visit someone else without her. I'd fashion a hiding place in my bag or behind the mattress of the bed I was to sleep in.

Every time I was given some food, I saved a little bit or took extra when no one was looking and hid it so I could come back to it later, maybe in the evening when I was off to bed or if I was alone during the day, which I often was, wherever I was and whatever I was doing.

I'd make sure to be alone, at least for a little while. Then I'd take my stash out and eat it as slowly as I could in tiny rations while thinking about absolutely nothing at all. Eating in that way was my favourite thing, but there was something to it that scared me as well. Upon reflection, it becomes clear to me how long this has been going on. It's almost unreal that I've spent so many years tormented by something I had no chance of escaping. Even as a small child I felt trapped by food; I was just unable to say anything or even think about it and also so sure that no one would understand because I thought no one's life was like mine.

—

I don't know what came first: the food that made me a prisoner of myself or was I already a prisoner and food helped me endure? Because it, or the mere thought of it, was there for me and gave me what I needed. Food and candy both enticed and frightened me. They haunted me and made it seem that I was never really free, so I liked seeing that other people could be as hungry and desirous as I was, or could at least appear to be.

Sometimes I hear people talk longingly about their childhood snacks, going to someone's house after school and eating cheese sandwiches and stirring up a glass of chocolate milk, and I loved that too. I loved snacking with classmates; snack time was a favourite meal because it reminded me of breakfast but didn't have a clear end point, but also because everyone else seemed to look forward to it as much as I did. They all seemed to be starving at that time of day and wanted to get home and eat as quickly as possible, and it made me feel a bit more normal. It was as if something loosed its grip on me when we walked into a friend's kitchen and started helping ourselves. As if I'd been chased around by some dangerous being for a long time and had finally found a haven.

In some homes there was nothing we wanted to eat, but we usually visited one of the kids who lived in a nice house by the lake below the school, and there they would have fruit and kefir and cereals, and bags of sandwich bread in the cupboards, the sort of thing my mother never bought because it was unhealthy and expensive, but even though there was so much, sometimes the parents would get angry because we'd drink all the milk or take too many slices of toast, and the thought of their anger preoccupied me so much that I couldn't really enjoy all that was at hand. I would have liked some assurance that we really were allowed to take what we wanted and no one would complain about us, because I never wanted to put a foot wrong and was so afraid that someone would be angry.

One of the working mothers always got home early in the afternoon. She would carry her bags into the house, which was filled with decorative objects and was always spic and span in a way that frightened me, and then she'd go into the kitchen and set them on the counter and start shouting and charging around in there. Usually we'd made sandwiches and a bowl of fruit kissel or maybe chocolate custard; when we finished eating, we'd clean up after ourselves and put the milk in the fridge and the dishes in the dishwasher, but we always forgot something or failed to do it properly. Bread crumbs, stains, a sticky spoon, or a rug that had been displaced in the dining room next to the kitchen. The mother would stand there, red in the face, screaming at us, and I kept thinking that she was like a monster, a beast set free. I couldn't understand how it was possible to be so angry with your child.

They kept a fully stocked fridge and a lot of food at home. I don't think she was overweight, but she certainly perceived herself as fat compared to how she would have liked to look, and maybe the reason I think of her sometimes was that twisted expression on her face, which was like the one I'd worn when I felt constrained by something indeterminate that took hold of me, and by everything in the kitchen, when I perceived that someone else had made a mess and assumed I'd be the one to clean up.

Moreover I'm under the impression that she actually worked with food in some capacity. I think she was a food writer or recipe developer and I can't help but think she probably had a difficult relationship with food. That's what started happening after my conversations with the people who had problems similar to mine. That's what I became. Somewhere deep down I knew I should take a more nuanced view, but either I felt lonely and misunderstood and thought no one else was like me or I'd see it everywhere: the tendencies with food and with other things, the hatred of the rest of the world, the feeling of being trapped, the unrealistic self-image, the victimhood, the manipulation, and the inability to express one's feelings honestly and set boundaries, before there was too much of everything – food or other people's desires and demands and advances.

I suppose I still find it hard to stop myself from diagnosing others in this way. It's like a shard in my eye that has been lodged there ever since I learned about addictive personalities in some course with American factual literature on addiction, where I sat in a circle with women, only women, from all over the country, many of whom had probably gravitated there mostly to get properly thin once and for all, and did not expect to be forced to question themselves, their behaviours and ways of being. At least I certainly hadn't wanted to do that.

—

After *Mastering the Art of French Cooking*, I found another cookbook that was not as exciting but that I liked nonetheless. It was also intended as a kind of guide to teach you everything you needed to know in the kitchen; vast, and thick, it was out on the big white table one day when my mother was looking for a red wine sauce recipe in it. My favourite chapter was on how to plan dinners: big parties or cheap everyday dinners for a family. I soaked up everything about how to stretch the food to feed many and how to take care of leftovers, plan your shopping according to the season, and vary the most affordable raw ingredients so that no one gets bored.

I read about the root vegetable family and the cabbage family and how to sprout peas and make a sourdough starter. In addition, there was an educational pictorial recipe for glace au four that I loved and read over and over again: first bake the sponge cake in a long pan and let it cool, then whip up the meringue and add fresh raspberries and two lengths of ice cream from the cardboard half-litre packets that were common at the time, which I knew siblings would cut down the middle, then each eat one half straight from the container. After that you would quickly cover the whole thing with the meringue batter, sprinkle it with almond flakes, and put it in the oven until the almonds and meringue got a little colour, to be served immediately of course. Speed was of the utmost importance so that the ice cream inside wouldn't get much chance to melt. In the photo, the festive dessert was in slices, the ice cream filling white and gleaming below the meringue, and there was something about the idea of making ice cream in the oven that I couldn't let go of. I loved anything that couldn't wait and had to be served right away, and when I think about it I still do.

I even read about aspic, presumably because it was so strange as well, and about onion soup au gratin, because it was exciting to imagine that lid of bread and cheese covering the soup and because it was a dish my mother had always talked about. They ate it at night when she was young, she said, it was a dish many people could afford and was served in all the pubs they frequented back then. Perhaps it made them feel in step with their time, with the student protests in Paris, while being cheap, filling, and easy to enjoy. Sweet, salty, and greasy.

During all the years I lived at home, I read cookbooks, and my mother and her boyfriend read them too. With him, she'd started to cook a lot more food. She cooked in a different way and her dishes were more time-consuming and complicated, she did more shopping than before and also seemed to eat a lot more, and not what she'd usually have when it was just the two of us. She no longer talked about everything she couldn't stomach, nor about good food as something that was somewhere other than where we were. Her boyfriend was clumsy in the kitchen and not particularly knowledgeable about cooking, but he enjoyed eating and drinking and buying food and wine, and the thought of failure didn't seem to frighten him at all. He'd try anything once.

I heard them laughing at Peking ducks that were full of air only to deflate the second they stuck a knife in or at soufflés that collapsed as they were taking them out of the oven and soups that tasted as if he'd dropped the salt shaker in. She stayed with him in the kitchen tasting sauces and stews and sighing loudly with pleasure. They would take a stack of cookbooks and carry them into her bedroom and lie there in bed for half the day talking about what they'd make for dinner in the evening, and what they'd have to drink with it. This was their world, which they were building together. The bright side of it, from my perspective. I could hear them from one end of the apartment to the other on many occasions. When they were cooking, there were low, delighted shouts about this or that and how it should taste, and I listened for the sounds of them getting happy and full of anticipation before heading into the city in his car to shop at the market hall there. For the rest of the weekend, the apartment would smell of wine and garlic, and I stayed in my room for longer and longer periods of time.

—

Because of all the recipes I was reading, I was learning more and more about cooking, but I had a hard time doing it when I was the only one who was going to eat, and even after my mother and her boyfriend moved in together, they usually ate home-cooked food only on weekends or when guests were coming. Or maybe I just remember it that way because I didn't like what they cooked, and I still didn't like him.

At first I could hardly stand the idea of her and me living with him, but when I realized we were moving to the city, to an apartment more than twice the size of ours, I didn't mind as much. I felt ice cold, but that's how I thought. I hated him as much as I had the first time I met him and I thought he smelled exactly as bad as he did then, but he was almost always at our place anyway, so it hardly mattered whether or not they were living together.

He said our new apartment was called a mansion flat. It had a separate kitchen entrance used in the past by the servants, the rooms had antique tiled stoves, and from the hallway there were long servants' corridors leading to the kitchen, which had a large walk-in pantry. The big white table fit inside, but that's not where we sat when we ate together. We'd sit at a long oak table that had belonged to his family. He'd sit on the short end and drink several glasses of wine with the food, and the wine made him babble; sometimes he broke into tears and started telling us about how he hadn't been allowed to sit at that table as a child, he had never been allowed to eat dinner with his mother and stepfather in their dining room when he was little – he had to sit in the kitchen with the cook and house girl. Or did he say 'maid'? Grandma had been a house girl herself and she'd said that was the term they used. He sat with the cook and the house girl because he did not have the same father as his siblings, and Sunday was the only day they made an exception and allowed him to join them in the dining room.

—

It might not have been like this, but I remember feeling we were always about to eat something I didn't like when we sat down at that old table, dishes that didn't feel like food one eats at home on an ordinary evening. Duck and game in various forms, that French onion soup, beef bourguignon with a strong smoky flavour from the lardons, fish fillets with shrimp and white wine sauce, dishes seasoned with rosemary and juniper berries, and roast lamb with potatoes au gratin or garlic butter that stank up the kitchen. There was a dishwasher in the kitchen, but most of what they used – the knives, the cast-iron pans, the crystal glasses from which they drank their red wine – could not be washed in the machine. It often took several days for it to fill up, and because my mother said not to start it until it was full, the dirty plates and cutlery that had been placed in there would start to smell. My mother's taste really changed once she started living with him. I was older now, and it seemed to me that she was more living with him than with me. She no longer avoided everything that was fatty, as she'd done before, and she didn't as often suggest we have sour milk for dinner, which I liked, or raw vegetables with boiled eggs and sprouts and cottage cheese. She wanted to eat meat just like he did and she thought I was making a show of it when the thought of eating animals made me sick.

One time when I came into the kitchen, they were standing there with a meat cleaver and a deer leg with bone and were examining the chuck and shank and looking in some book for instructions on how to cut it up. I made a noise of disgust when I saw the skinned piece of meat, and then she lifted it up in front of her and moved it in a way that made it seem like the leg was leaping into the air, and I felt my stomach churn.

I was disgusted by the dishwasher and by their food, but even more so by him. I had been from the start, disgust mixed with fear, but when the three of us lived together I got to see him in even sharper relief. When he ate, his champing made me shudder, he spilled a lot and often had food around his mouth, and I remember thinking it was strange because, coming from a nice family, he surely would have been taught better table manners.

The worst was seeing him eating in the kitchen the day after they'd hosted a party, or when he'd gone out to various pubs with their friends the night before. Wearing only his underwear, he'd eat leftover meat with his fingers straight out of the fridge, or herring or something prepared with sprats that Mom had put in there. He'd drink beer from the can, and the sound of his eating and the smell of his body and what he was gobbling up would make me turn right around and go back to my room. His stench of stale alcohol and something rotten that I'd hated at first whiff.

—

He never ate breakfast, which is what I wanted to eat more than anything, all day long if I could. I wanted cold, sweet food and plenty of it. As soon as I got home from school, I'd take out a bowl and fill it with mild plain yogourt and cereal or muesli and go sit on the floor in their bedroom. If I looked out one of the windows there, I'd sometimes see a fat man in one of the apartments in the building opposite. He'd sit at his kitchen table and eat for hours on end some days, evening or night. I watched him often. He sat with the ceiling light on and his face turned toward the window, so my view of him was plain and clear; I watched him sit there, get up and go to the fridge, and then sit back down at the table, and I could see he was a person who had chosen food. He'd said no to life and everything going on there and decided to eat instead.

I fully understand this decision, but I don't recall what I thought about it at the time.

It was titillating to stand by the window and watch him eat, but I don't remember reflecting on the fact that I was engaged in the same thing. Almost every afternoon I would sit on the floor in that bedroom and eat while watching episodes of American soap operas that my mother and everyone else I knew despised. We had cable TV, her boyfriend was rarely home when she wasn't, and her new job meant she was often on the road. I ate a bowl of yogourt and then another and another, and when I was finished it struck me that some chocolate would be really good right now. My mother's boyfriend loved chocolate, so she'd keep chocolate bars in one of the high cabinets in the pantry, where, when the building was constructed, it was thought that the cook or the house girl would fetch crockery and cutlery in order to set the table in the dining room.

I knew I should have been more interested in the liquor bottles that were on a special shelf in there, or high up in some other cabinet, or tucked away behind the laundry basket in the walk-in closet or somewhere else, but I didn't touch them. I only took chocolate, or was thinking about taking it. If I saw that a wrapper had been opened, I went back again and again and snapped a little piece off each time, if it was a chocolate bar from the store I might take the whole thing for myself, but if she'd just come back from a trip and had bought something less common on the plane, maybe Swiss milk chocolate with rum raisins or a giant Toblerone, I did everything I could not to open it and take a bite.

—

I knew she was saving the chocolate for her boyfriend in the same way she was saving her biscuits for when she was free to sit at the big white table and drink tea and read. I knew she'd intended for them to have chocolate one night after dinner, when they'd be sitting on the couch together drinking more wine or whisky or something else he liked, revelling in how good they had it. Sometimes I'd hear him say as much to her, We've got it good, don't we?, and then he'd bury his face in her neck and kiss her.

And I really made an effort to leave the chocolate be.

I moved around the kitchen buffet and wished she'd take it out spontaneously and ask me if I wanted some. When she didn't, I knew I'd soon give up and see my own fingers scurrying around the stash like hungry little rats. And in the same way, I always thought I'd have only one bowl of yogourt, but each time I'd take a second helping and then a third right after, as if I had no control over my own movements. The people I usually talk to say that getting used to constantly breaking promises to yourself makes you lose your sense of boundaries and feel ashamed, which was true. I couldn't say no, neither to others nor to myself, but as long as I was eating, it wasn't a problem because I could push away everything that came with it, I could disconnect or at least endure every unpleasant emotion and thought and even the feeling of being too full, which I had previously hated.

Sometimes I ate the chocolate a bit at a time in secret until it ran out or until there was only a little left for them, and when my mother went to fetch it from the buffet when they were getting cozy, I'd hear her let out a surprised cry in the hallway. If she asked me if I'd eaten it, I said no and let the silence take over. I didn't know how to tell her that I couldn't stop eating, that the chocolate had found its way inside me and made me lie and do other things. It turned me into a bad person, but on the other hand this was how I'd always felt anyway.

⁓

This was toward the end of my childhood. I wanted nothing more than to grow up and have my own home, my own kitchen with my own food, and my own friends who could come and eat it. Friends I could cook dinner for. But at the same time, I feared everything that went with it, everything to which a person my age was supposed to aspire. I'd so dearly wanted to grow up, but as adulthood drew near, I couldn't imagine how it was supposed to proceed and how I'd be able to handle everything it demanded.

On many days, I wanted nothing more than to sit like that in front of the television, on the floor of my mother's bedroom, swallowing spoonful after spoonful of cool yogourt, or standing in the servants' hallway with my hand in the buffet, gorging on chocolate and hoping no one would walk through the door and discover me. This way of eating made me feel like a child again, or at least like someone who couldn't do anything and of whom no one could expect anything. If the phone rang in my room, I let it go until the rings died out, and when the caller asked me at school the next day what I'd been up to, I made up something that sounded good and didn't lead to further questions. It was also true that I couldn't actually do other things while I was eating: I couldn't talk, I couldn't go out, I couldn't study or do anything else I knew I should be doing, and I thought it felt so good, as if I'd shut myself off.

—

All these years later, what follows seems so alien and strange I can barely remember how it came to pass, but I think it was around then that I started to compensate for some of what I was eating by getting rid of it. I'd read somewhere, probably long before, that there were women who induced vomiting to stay thin. I didn't do this every day or each time I overate, but only once in a while when I felt like I had to play it safe. After all, I wasn't that man across the street; part of me still wanted to be an attractive young woman with a fantastic life ahead of me.

But even then I couldn't identify with being a person who'd throw up what she'd eaten. Can anyone? I've understood that for some people it seems to fit in naturally with their idea of femininity, yet another given among the many things that are part of being a woman, but not for me. On the contrary, my sense was that I was supposed to be independent of those stereotypes. I wouldn't be one of those women or girls, I would make use of the life and the freedom I'd been given. The people with whom I spent my time never discussed subjects such as weight or diet-ing. We weren't like that, the description of a young woman's life in a society where our bodies could sell anything didn't seem to apply to us, and maybe that's what made doing what I did so easy. It was as if I wasn't the one sitting on the floor in front of the toilet throwing up, but a different person – I didn't know who she was or where she'd come from.

Where did this come from?

I'd also never perceived my mother or grandmother as women who wanted to try to get their bodies to conform. They didn't talk about how to look pleasing and be beautiful or even healthy and neat, and I gleaned that it was my responsibility not to care about such things either, however so much indicated that I should. I felt ashamed that my body didn't look the way everything suggested it should, but I felt even more ashamed for feeling ashamed. My mother and grandmother never expressed any such dissatisfaction, not in words anyway, but why would they have escaped this? The research on eating disorders shows that the exclusion of certain foods – including meat – can be a symptom, and it has also been found that eating disorders are genetically determined. They are not only the result of circumstances in the psychosocial envi-ronment, but also have their foundations in biology – genetic factors that are passed on.

As for my father, I hadn't seen much of him since I vomited tagliatelle and bolognese all over his beautiful kitchen. Rereading letters from him that I saved, ones he sent me in the following years, I can see now that he'd written more than once about having a guest room and it being empty most of the time. He constantly made such remarks in his letters, hints and more or less obvious suggestions, but I didn't notice at the time because I didn't want to see him.

The idea of it made me too nervous. The year after I turned eighteen, I travelled with a friend to the city where he lived. I had a cellphone, my mom had given him the number without first asking me because she could probably tell I was avoiding him, and he called to insist we meet up because so much time had passed. There was something demanding in his voice that I didn't recognize and I could tell I wouldn't be able to get out of it this time. Talking to him still terrified me. I didn't know what to say. I had to think everything through and I kept trying to find a way of speaking that would make me seem impeccable in his eyes.

Yes, I think I was seeking impeccability. I wanted to convey that I was a person without flaws, and I wanted to be one in all other contexts as well. I wanted to be able to handle anything and never put a foot wrong. I've heard people in my treatment program talking about that kind of thing too – the difficulty of admitting you're wrong or the importance of being right about everything, all the time. They say it comes naturally to people like us. It was nonetheless taxing, of course, but especially because I knew how impossible it was for me to appear flawless before someone like him – me, the person who hadn't even been able to eat the food he'd cooked for me.

I couldn't get out of seeing him, but this time he wanted to have dinner out and it was less intimidating than being at his house. He gave me the name of a restaurant near the office where he worked, in a neighbourhood I'd read had the most expensive real estate in the world. It was an early spring evening, and outside were men dressed in camel-hair ulsters, drinking drinks and smoking cigars. They turned their heads in my direction as I approached, and one of them opened the door for me and held it. They were looking at me in a way that made me not know whether to feel exalted or embarrassed.

He sat facing the door so that our eyes met as I crossed the threshold. It was a small restaurant with brick walls, white-painted wood panels, and elegant dishes being discreetly carried to the tables. We drank champagne to start and he ordered an appetizer, a main course, and wine for both of us. He went there often, I realized. I looked at his hands holding the glasses and cutlery, and his mouth as it moved. It was so strange to imagine – the way he lived his life. I was very hungry because I hadn't eaten anything all day, I'd waited because I knew he'd pick up the bill, but I only managed a quick look at the menu before he ordered and it was taken away from me, I couldn't see what anything cost because there were no prices. What I remember is the crab salad with watercress and candied almonds, which he said was always on the menu and he was sure I'd like it. I'd never eaten any of these things, except crab of course, the ones we fished out of the sea on long lines and roasted live in the fire. When there were other children on the island, we ate the crab in hot dog buns their mothers brought, but I'd never eaten crab meat scraped out and put in a salad.

He seemed like a different person that night and I felt different too. It was easier to tell him things and he was also more talkative. It was as if he were closer to me. Maybe it was the champagne and all the cold, pale rosé that arrived later that did it, or the sticky candied almonds in my salad, but as I sat there chatting with him and noticing that the wait staff was treating me like his girlfriend and not his daughter, I thought it was because I'd grown up. He wasn't used to children, but it didn't matter anymore because I'd become an adult, I thought.

—

I'd started working and earning money and had my own apartment, with my own kitchen and my own cookbooks. I bought food and invited people over for dinner and tried out recipes. They still conferred a sense of peace, but they also made me feel like a new person. There was something about buying and owning expensive cookbooks and household items that made me feel unlike myself, like a person who could take care of herself, who knew who she was and how she wanted things to be.

In the kitchen, I was in control of everything that was going on. I loved to think of myself as a grown woman who enjoyed cooking, especially for others. My food would draw praise and I took pleasure in that, seeing the change in people's faces as they ate what I'd cooked for them. I loved how food could be a way of controlling other people's emotions too and I loved everything there was to do in the kitchen. But at the same time I was ashamed of it, of my embarrassing attraction to the home, to what was considered maternal and feminine, and to the old conventions of femininity. I was aware of this, like I was aware that I wasn't meant to put myself down physically or in any other way, as women have always done, that the last thing I was meant to become was a housewife.

—

Once I'd learned more about different cooking methods and became more confident in the kitchen, I felt emboldened to serve more complicated dishes and to cook for more people, and I noticed that cooking, apart from everything else, also offered a kind of protection. Cooking for others was an opportunity to participate and yet not, to spend time together while keeping your distance. It was a way to create something that others could share and that seemed to make them happy and sometimes even moved them, made them tell me about food they'd cooked themselves, about trips they'd taken or unforgettable meals they'd eaten as children, and it made me feel close to them.

This would allow something of myself to find its way inside other people, and simply talking about food could have the same effect. Back then, food and gastronomy or everyday cooking had not yet become common topics of conversation; telling others what you'd eaten and what kind of food you liked to eat or cook was still considered odd, and I liked getting into those conversations because they seemed to reveal what was otherwise invisible.

It was entirely possible, for example, to sit at a dinner table and eat with virtual strangers, but if you also started talking about food, an almost undue intimacy would emerge. I sought this out and began to think that anyone who thought about or cooked food in the way that I did, who read about food or searched for food or placed importance on what they ate, was similar to me somehow. I didn't think anyone else could be as grotesque and weak as I was, but I felt a sense of recognition.

And if they weren't like me, I still find myself wondering, how was that possible? All the people who eat and cook and in various ways are involved with food, but entirely lack my own immoderation and senselessness when it comes to eating – how can they love food and not feel that all they want is to lock themselves away with it, never to emerge again?

—

I've found myself thinking that all lovers of food must be abandoned children because, in most families anyway, food is the only thing within reach for a child who can't handle all that it means to exist. I watch children in cooking programs shuck scallops and whip up béarnaise sauces and I wonder how they're doing, because I so easily forget that there are other dimensions to food. The excess is so nonchalant it manages to obscure the fact that food is as strong a symbol of prosperity as ever. Being fat is no longer associated with status and power. However, a reliable flow of good, well-made food is.

And for some, food is no more than food. For a long time this notion was incomprehensible to me. People who didn't care what they ate and how it tasted confused me and made me feel forlorn, as if I'd been flung into a great void. Yet I envied them because, in my eyes, they were free.

Personally, I felt insecure without food or what I felt about it. If I was visiting someone or travelling somewhere, I'd worry there'd be nothing I'd want to eat, and if I was at a party or dinner where food was being treated poorly, it bothered me. If the food was unappetizing or if someone ate too quickly and without consideration, it would make me sad, and it was different from the usual melancholy about the transience of things that people sometimes talk about, the idea that you might think long and hard about a particular dish and imagine it, figure out how to make it and get everything you need, cook and set the table, only to watch it all disappear in an instant.

When I did the cooking, I loved to watch people throw themselves into eating because the food was delicious. I wanted them to not be able to wait to eat my food and I could eat that way too, but I never did in company. I was alone in those moments and it was a different kind of hunger that drove me then, one that belonged to the movement that preceded it, that grabbed hold of me each time and held me in its grip until all I could do was eat, stuffing myself far too full.

—

If food was not given the role in the world that it had inside me, I sensed a rising desolation. As if there was nothing there, no love, no history, no family. But the opposite was probably true. For many years I thought food filled my existence, but the truth was that it slowly but surely was draining it of everything.

I'd so longed for a home of my own where I could make my own decisions, and I'd thought that if I could just have that, my loneliness would disappear. Then I'd be alone for the simple reason that I was a young person who'd recently left home, living alone, like so many others. But it was hard to go out and buy food and go back to the apartment to cook and eat it; there was something about sitting there on my own with a plate in front of me that brought about a familiar ache in my stomach. Eating alone still felt sad, and that caught me off-guard.

It's not like anyone had been telling me what to do and what not to do before, but when I had my own home all bets were off. Most of the time I didn't cook for myself, but when I came home after being out late, I had to eat. I'd be so hungry I didn't have the energy to feel sorry for myself. I drank milk and ate ice cream and spongy white bread I'd bought for a few kronor at the convenience store on the way home.

I knew what I wanted and how it would make me feel, and if it didn't work, I'd get restless and feel unsatisfied. Predictability is something that has been, evolutionarily speaking, an important part of the human biological experience of eating, which is said to be one reason why many people like food with a crunch to it – because crunchiness, like the freshness of food in general, is a characteristic that can be predicted at a glance. Reliability was part of the attraction for me, and I thought I could feel something primal taking over when I ate. As if something inherited set in, other than the fact that I hungered to be filled.

I had turned to food because it gave me everything I wanted and needed, but the older I got, the clearer it became how short-lived the effect was. It surged and then subsided, a security and a warmth that ultimately existed only in the brief, flashing moments when my mouth was full. Around those moments was emptiness. And my eating made me even more isolated than I already was, because I could always find – or thought I could find – my comfort there, I never had to be confronted with anything real. I didn't have to speak up when someone hurt me or get to the bottom of things that felt difficult, thus perpetuating my inability to exist.

—

There were times when my mother called to ask me to come over and taste something she thought I should learn how to eat, foie gras or some particularly fine oysters or beluga caviar once when she'd been given a tin as a present. It had been flown in on ice, she said, and she'd bought a particular kind of white wine for us to drink because it tasted better than champagne. Best would have been to drink ice-cold vodka with it, she said, but that's not what we were going to do.

She was still living with the man she loved. They often had parties and dinners with much wine and many courses, and sometimes they'd invite me and, if there was something special to celebrate, my friends as well. And even though I no longer lived there, I carried the keys to the apartment with me wherever I went. I'd go there sometimes when they weren't at home, and also when they were. It was so big and the rooms so far apart that my presence was hardly noticeable. I'd go into the kitchen and find something to eat and sit down with it at the big white table. My mother's French shortbread with dark chocolate, a piece of cave-aged Gruyère, a packet of figs if there was nothing else, and when I sat there I could breathe a sigh of relief because I was hidden away and beyond the reach of everything and everyone.

I didn't know it was possible to leave your body to the extent that I did that night, after I'd made my daughter the rice pudding and tried to get her to taste it. There I was, floating beneath our ceiling, the great eye above the two of us on the floor by the big white table. And an eye was what I'd always been, I'd seen everything around me, but this was the first time I was seeing my adult self in all its pettiness. How small I was next to her, under her little hand moving across my back.

What happened next and how I came out of that mute, paralyzed state I can no longer remember, but somehow the evening ended. I picked myself up off the floor and went into the bathroom with her and brushed her teeth and put her to bed, stroking her hair and singing to her until she fell asleep, and then I must have fallen asleep too because when I woke back up it was dark and the night sky inky and deep beyond the window.

The darkness seemed to press itself against the panes as if it wanted to break in, and on the table our plates and the baking pan with the rice pudding remained. I felt hungry even though not many hours had passed since we'd eaten. I got up and sat in her chair and ate up her leftovers. I plated some more and ate that too. I'd only intended to eat the one extra helping, no more, but when I'd eaten up I didn't feel satisfied. Strangely, I was starving.

I kept eating, and as I ate I thought something was happening. It still didn't taste the way I remembered, but I took another bite and another and concentrated on the saltiness, the sweetness, and the silky softness in my mouth, all that was there nonetheless, and then I was filled with something at once effervescent and calm, a sense of wholeness that came from the movement of lips touching the grains of rice, jaw working, and hand holding the fork going up and down between my mouth and the plate. Little by little, everything began to make sense. All my thoughts seemed to dissolve and the evening sailed slowly away.

I ate the last of it straight from the baking pan, leaning forward and holding one of its thick handles. I thought about Grandma and

Grandad and how they'd sat in their chairs with the freshly baked rice pudding between them, Grandad furthest in and Grandma closest to the kitchen so she could easily fetch anything that might be missing, something he realized he wanted or something she thought I might need. We would want for nothing by way of food. More milk, another slice of bread. Some salt. I remembered the electric heat of their apartment and the smell of them everywhere, their skin and hair and bodies, dust and sugar cookie crumbs, their perpetually dark-rimmed nails. Perhaps because they so often had their fingers in the earth, in the potted plants and balcony boxes in winter and in the countryside in the summer. And I remembered how certain relatives would eye my nails when they came to visit, and led me to the bathroom to scrub the dirt away.

I pictured the steam juicer hissing on the stove, downy piles of elder that Grandad had picked along the street and in the park, and the demijohn in which he fermented his wine. Was it made of dandelion or maybe sloe? Wasn't he constantly foraging, just like Grandma? I thought about everything they said that I never heard – and still have never heard – anyone else say, I thought about the view of the shopping centre and the other tall buildings, and about the prepackaged 'ice cream boat' sundae Grandma left on the oilcloth to thaw a little and that I gobbled up according to a method I'd established the very first time I was served one. Chocolate-covered ice cream waves like dark molars in a row.

—

It wasn't possible to recreate a dish and make it taste like it did in my memory, like it had in childhood, which seemed so distant now that I had a child of my own, even though it really wasn't, even though it still held me in such a firm grip. And it wasn't possible for me to be the parent I wanted to be. It wasn't as easy as I thought it would be, to give your child what you wanted to give them. I thought about all the things I hadn't said and all the things I hadn't done, all my silences, absences and deficiencies that appeared in such sharp relief as I sat there, alone at the big white table.

In the end, nothing was left of the rice pudding. I hadn't saved any of it for my daughter; I'd eaten it all myself, polished it all off without her having taken a single bite. I had the feeling that my insatiability had devoured all that was around and inside me. Nothing had come of all that I'd intended to give her. I looked at the dish, as good as empty but for what was stuck on the edges where I hadn't been able to properly spread the butter, or rather had not taken enough care.

Was it the same with everything? Was that the mother I was?

I got up and went to the kitchen. I felt a rush as I opened the cabinet and took out a packet of rice cakes that was sitting there. I popped one in my mouth and chewed it while running my eyes along the shelves. The white quinoa, almond flour, and oatmeal, jars of butter beans and chickpeas and borlotti beans, and whole peeled tomatoes and artichoke bottoms. Honey, various hot sauces and ketchup and salsa and soy, tuna in olive oil, soba and udon noodles, miso paste, rice paper, aborio rice, and sheets of nori. Black garlic and unsulfured dried apricots. Alphabet pasta in different colours, which she didn't like but I kept them anyway because I liked the look of the package. I liked buying that kind of thing, imported organic products with packaging that I thought was nice, that was meant to appeal to children.

—

My eyes caught on the bag containing the large loaf of sourdough I'd bought for breakfast the next day but had to give my daughter some of after she refused to eat the rice pudding. I took it out and put it on the counter and cut a few thick slices, took a couple of tomatoes from their dish and butter and a cheese from the fridge and thought about the cheese sandwiches of my childhood, the ones I sometimes got in the swimming pool cafeteria or on the train if there were delays and the lunch Grandma had packed in the plastic boxes with the snap-on lids was not enough. They'd be spread with so much butter it made me sick. They'd be lined up close together in their plastic wrap, the butter in a single lump between the cheese and the soft white bread, and a thin slice of tomato on top.

The way the tomato made the butter and cheese moist, clashing with its freshness, was repulsive to me, but now I could taste how the richness and saltiness of the butter and cheese married the sweetness of a tomato slice. I'd grown to like it, love it even, and couldn't get enough. I ate the first sandwich standing up leaning over the kitchen counter, I couldn't wait, and by the time I'd made another and bitten into it, shiny peach-pink tomato juice was running down the side of my hand and forearm. I licked it off and kept on eating, I ate more and more, and then managed to hold back only so as to give myself enough time to make several sandwiches and put them on a plate and carry it to the big white table. I was going to sit down so I could really enjoy it, I thought. That's how it would go. I'd do everything in my power to relive the memory of a pleasure, even though I knew it was impossible, I always hoped to sense something close to the satisfaction I'd felt the first few times, but however much I wanted this, it wouldn't work. I'd find myself in something else, a different tempo.

It was almost as if eating was a task to be completed, like something I had to dispose of. In the 1970s, a famous American psychoanalyst wrote that for the compulsive eater, food must be eaten quickly because it is like a threat or danger that must be neutralized. Once consumed, the crisis is over and what remains are the overeater's usual feelings of guilt and shame.

I opened my mouth and inserted my sandwiches one by one, chewed and swallowed, hardly feeling anything. It went by fast, as if in a single inhalation, and when they were gone, I looked into the darkness outside the window. I could hear drunken people moving between the pubs on the hill, and sirens somewhere in the far distance, but between me and all the familiar sounds of the night was a dullness. Everything I'd eaten had dampened my senses, but that was what I'd intended: to be inundated in one moment and released from everything the next. A moment in which nothing existed and there was no feeling.

That's what I was looking for, I think, to be switched on and off and reach that moment of emptiness that seemed able to fuse all the disparate parts of me and obliterate everything else. I can't explain it in any other way. It was like a wordless movement pulling me along toward its completion, grabbing hold of me again and again and forcing me to let go of everything else. Something shifted in me when this happened, a stiffness came over me as if from behind, and made me hold my breath.

—

I caught sight of my cellphone lying on the big white table. A text message from my daughter's father, asking why I never picked up when he called, and when I read those words it struck me that I should probably eat some ice cream too. Wouldn't that be delicious right now? And if I did that, I'd also be able to clear myself out more easily, so I left the chair and went into the kitchen and opened the freezer, but there was no ice cream. I must have eaten it up one night in the past week when I'd come home alone. I still liked eating at night because I felt like no one was watching me and I didn't care about minding my manners and taking care of myself.

My daughter was asleep in her bed, her arms stretched above her head as my grandmother had taught me a child should sleep, she told me I used to sleep like that and it was how you knew children felt safe and secure, she said. I would only be gone for a short time. I put on a coat and went out the door, down the stairs, and into the late-night shop on the corner. The hour was late and people were crowding inside. At the counter the smell of cigarette smoke and cheap perfumes mingled with the haze of the chain store's grilled 'Italian' sandwiches, so called because they had some kind of mortadella on them, and their unnaturally red sausages rolling on the roller grill slicked with glossy frying grease. The whole scene disgusted me, the sight of all the drunk people in there shopping for something vile, the men's slurring voices, the laughter, and the women's shrill little shouts. All the skin on display even though it was so biting cold and how they stuffed it all down, spilling and screaming at each other with food in their mouths.

I kept my eyes down as I walked to the freezer chest in the middle of the store and quickly, and without even really needing to look up, took out a box of six ice creams. On it was a woman's sensual half-open mouth, her full lips painted with a lipstick that gleamed against the chocolate her teeth were biting into, exposing the ice cream underneath. I went to the cash register without looking around, paid, and slipped out with the box under my arm. Everyone in there must have been too drunk to notice what I was buying, I thought, and even if they had seen me, no one would have cared. It was only in my mind that my actions and I were at the centre of everything.

—

I hurried along the sidewalk, and as I walked through the building door I thought I heard a noise. It sounded like a child crying. I'd sneaked out of the apartment very quietly and listened at the front door after closing it. I'd reasoned that she would not wake up in the short time I'd be gone, but how could I have been so sure? Something could have woken her up by now. Maybe she'd had a nightmare or been woken by a noise or felt a pain somewhere. The crying grew louder and louder in my mind, and I imagined her in the hallway with our door wide open, the big white table and chairs and a glimpse of the rest of the apartment behind her. Tears streaming down her cheeks and her face contorted by the sobbing.

I usually took the stairs, but this time I threw myself into the elevator, keys in hand. When I got out on our floor, it was silent. I entered the apartment and saw her in bed just as I had left her, sleeping in exactly the same position. I tore off my clothes on the way to the bed and let them drop to the floor in a trail behind me before I lay down between the sheets next to the cold box. The first ice cream was still hard when I ate it and so was the second. I didn't have time to let them thaw and I knew the third would now have the perfect consistency. By the time I started eating it, the chocolate had softened, making the flavour more distinct. There were double layers of dark chocolate with a smeary caramel in between and I forced the tip of my tongue down there. I slowed my eating, already feeling very full, and by the time I took the next ice cream out of the box and peeled off the wrapper, it had begun to melt and the sweet white chocolate coating yielded the second my teeth touched it. Its interior slipped right down as I sucked on the ice cream, it dripped down my cheek and I had to lick my lips and chin. A pleasant heaviness settled inside me and I rested my head on the pillow, while I held the ice cream stick in front of my mouth and let my tongue envelop what was left. I lay there, and everything else evaporated. There was silence inside me. I felt nothing, perceived nothing.

—

I don't know how long I lay like that. I kept slipping from slumber into sleep and I had to force myself to get up. In the bathroom, I took my toothbrush and squatted in front of the toilet. In a way I wanted to get fat, I wanted to turn into a giant woman who couldn't leave the house and who would have to be removed by hoisting crane when she died. That was already how I felt, I both feared it and yearned for it. But I also knew it wasn't allowed. I opened my mouth and pressed the toothbrush handle against the side of my throat. Afraid I'd waited too long, I poked around with the handle until I found exactly the right spot and felt the familiar irritation in my throat, felt the juices releasing and waves travelling through the lower part of my torso until it all rushed up my throat and a thick mucus settled in the toilet. I did it again and again until I sensed there was nothing left, and then I got up, washed off the toothbrush, rinsed my mouth, and brushed my teeth, carefully so as not to damage the enamel.

Afterwards, I looked at myself in the bathroom mirror, into my teary eyes. I felt stupid standing in front of the mirror like that, but I could never not do it. It was as if I had to stand there and stare at myself to understand that this was me – my mouth, my face, my body. Otherwise I didn't see it that way. I was not inside myself when I ate that way or when I got rid of what I'd eaten. It was my physical form that bought the food and went home and ate and threw it up, but it never felt like my real self was there when it happened. My self disappeared and I guess that's why I enjoyed it all so much.

—

I was able to throw up because I was detached from my body and my own will, but this detachment also isolated me from the vomiting, so much so that now, in retrospect, I can barely remember this. It's like something I've repressed or never acknowledged. But I do know that I stood there and looked at my face in the mirror afterward, and when I was done I took the last two ice creams and threw them in the garbage, then I went back to bed and began to fall asleep.

But with the first tug of sleep, it was as if I was again awakened and seized by a force that came from outside but was more than familiar. I went to the kitchen and opened the garbage cabinet and picked up the ice cream that was on top. It was soft and heavy but still seemed to have its integrity inside the wrapping paper. I could already taste it in my mouth and I knew I could do it again. I tore open the wrapper and was just about to put the damp half-melted chocolate in my mouth and let everything inside flow down my throat when a bottle of dish soap caught my eye. I'd read that some people poured dish soap on their food to stop themselves from eating it. I put the ice cream back in the garbage, picked up the other one and unwrapped it too, took the bottle, squirted dishwashing liquid on both of them, and went back to bed.

When I woke up the next morning, the pain writhed through me like a long black snake. It was an incontestable fact that each day was a new day, whatever my thoughts or feelings about it. The air around me felt impenetrable, as if I couldn't move if I tried, and my daughter was sleeping right up against me with her arm over mine. She must have crawled into my bed and lay down next to me during the night. I sat up, carefully so as not to wake her, gathered the ice cream wrappers left on the bed, put them in the empty cardboard box, and stuffed it in a bag I tied up and put outside the front door so she wouldn't see it.

I cleared away the dishes and everything else left over from the night, in the kitchen and on the big white table, and as I moved I noticed that my hands had curled and clenched. That's what would happen to me, I'd get tense and hardly breathed and my fingers would turn into claws. My whole body became hard and I felt as if someone were standing behind me, watching my every move. I took out the remaining crust of bread and made two small sandwiches, which I put on a tray. I opened the fridge and took out a jar of marmalade we'd made from ripe plums from a garden that belonged to a few friends. It flowed smoothly over the butter and had a redolent tang, the colour like candy gummies and wild winter apples.

When I was done, I put everything away as quickly as I could and, without breathing in the scent of the bread or looking at the shiny waves of butter softening in the tub, I wiped up all the crumbs on the counter until the kitchen looked tidy again and rinsed my hands, and when I turned around she was standing right in front of me, in her pyjamas, sleep still wrapped around her like a blanket. I handed her the breakfast tray and let her carry it to the table and then I went back to bed. I caught a glimpse of my body against the sheet before I pulled the comforter over me and saw that it resembled a rooting sow's, the pink of my skin against the bedding and the shape of my hips and thighs.

—

After a while I heard her. Is there more sandwich? she asked. I swallowed. I had a foul taste in my mouth, my throat burned and my head felt heavy, my whole body was heavy and stiff in that way. No, I said. It sounded like she was going to ask why, so I repeated myself; she was silent and asked if I was going to eat as well and I said no once more and thought of all the other questions that would come, all the things she would want to have and do, and how hard it would be to get through the day as it was. Again I saw myself so clearly, how I had lain there on the floor next to her, still and silent even though I wanted to touch her and say something.

I forced myself out of bed and into the kitchen and took the dish brush and scrubbed the pan with the traces of rice pudding baked onto it that I'd left to soak in the sink. The water had loosened the stuck bits and washing the pan was easy. It was an ordinary, slightly dented stainless-steel baking pan, nothing like my grandmother's. Neither my mother nor my grandmother had ever raised their voices at me, but I'd screamed at my daughter like an utter lunatic. I put the pan on the washing rack and wondered what Grandma had been so angry about that time she stood at the sink with the dinner dishes and smashed her china.

What did it mean? Perhaps her burst of anger was nothing like mine, but she too was a person who rarely said no and never got angry with anyone. Unless the anger was of the right kind, she'd swallow it when it did arise, and I'd thought that was part of what made her so wonderful. Despite everything else I was taught by my mother and her friends, I thought it was great to be a woman, a mother, who was mild and soft and perpetually available and never said no to anything. Throughout the late afternoon and evening before, I'd stayed by my daughter's side, pushed her in the stroller when she was too tired to walk, sat with her on the bus and subway without getting annoyed or even once losing my patience. Whatever she'd thrown out of her stroller I'd reached for, each time she refused something I'd comforted and coaxed her. I'd made sure to fulfill all her needs as I perceived them, and to follow her every whim because the opposite seemed almost physically impossible. And if someone greeted me or approached me in another manner, I'd have appeared as inviting and receptive as ever. It was like a reflex. Nonetheless the anger had come, and it struck with such force it had annihilated me.

～

Like my grandmother's, the original rice pudding would not have been a dessert but a main course or side dish when it was served at courts throughout Europe in the Middle Ages. Many hundreds of years later, when rice became cheap, rice pudding was often made in school cafeterias and hospitals, and when the dish had a renaissance in big-city restaurants around the world, the explanation was the modern human's longing for simplicity.

Whether or not my grandmother's cooking could be described as simple, her baking was more involved. When I was young, she made various kinds of small cookies as well as fruit and berry pies with decorated pie crusts; she froze parfaits, frosted sugar cookies, and braided sweet bread. And every time she told me it was time to bake, when she read a recipe aloud, whisked a batter, or took her steaming trays out of the oven, I felt something shift in her kitchen. It was as if something else entered and transformed it and us, giving everything a certain shine.

I was determined not to miss my mother when she left me with them, but it was hard. During the Christmas holidays when it was cold outside and dark in the early afternoon, I missed her even more than in the summer and the other times of the year. During the Christmas days themselves she was there, but then she'd leave and I'd have to stay. When we arrived, Grandma would have already hung a wreath on the door and decorated the hallway for Christmas with a gingerbread house she'd baked for me. On the low table under the hall mirror, everything that was usually there had been removed, and when I came in, a miniature winter wonderland would spread out before me, right at eye level.

When I was older, I started looking at it more closely, examining all the details and trying to see what she had done, how she'd created a landscape that seemed to have a life of its own. In the centre stood a stone church with a slate roof and bell tower and a small lamp lit inside; next to it was a lake, and on the other side a forest and a small house, the gingerbread walls of which she had glued together with melted sugar. She'd installed little gelatin leaf windows in the walls, royal icing was the snow on the roof, and a cotton candy smoke rose from the chimney. Every year something new about her methods was revealed to me – the lake was a shaving mirror she'd placed there, the reeds were made of straw she had gathered, and the snowdrifts were of the same cotton wadding she drowned in an onion concentrate and stuffed into my ears when they ached. Everywhere were tiny figures, yarn gnomes, straw angels, and little trolls climbing on the roof or playing in the snow or sledding on the ice. And on top of it all was a thin layer of fresh snow, icing sugar that she'd sifted over them.

—

Each year, Mom reminded me that there was no telling how much longer Grandma would have it in her to bake the gingerbread house and bring out the church and arrange it all. She told me this so I'd be prepared, and I got into the habit of watching Grandma closely right as I arrived, but after a few days I'd forget all about it because there was no indication that she was about to die or become too old or sick to do all the things she did.

She fried her rosettes, baked almond shells and brittle and toffee and several trays of gingerbread and saffron bread, and I thought that she'd made such an effort because she enjoyed it. And that the work you did in your own home was not a chore, because it was yours. Despite everything I'd heard about women's lives and lack of freedom, I thought this was particular to her, not what was expected of women in her time – being happy and available, arranging and decorating everything.

Every night during the Christmas holidays, she would take out a golden box, a big heavy box of chocolates that she said belonged to Grandad. You could tell how special it was by the look on her face and the way she carried it to the coffee table. Just to think, they send one every year, she said. Every year for thirty years! It was a present from the superstore where he'd worked after he left the railroad, it was after they'd gotten married and had children, and travelling as much as he did became difficult. I recognized the name of the store, he'd talked about it often, and I thought how pleased they must have been with him to send such a nice Christmas present every year.

I also knew that his foot had been crushed there while on the job. He'd gotten it stuck under a pallet and it had broken into thirty-two pieces, I think it was thirty-two anyway, but after an operation he made a full recovery and was able to go back to work as usual. An exemplary employee who was always on site and on time, always diligent and friendly. The chocolate box was a reminder of this, and another arrived one day when they were looking after me at our home and suddenly his foot swelled up so much he couldn't walk on it. The skin split into an open wound out of which whitish pus seeped. Grandma howled when she saw it and I didn't know what to say or where to go. I'd never seen him in pain and he didn't let on that he was then either, but you could see that one of the little bones under the skin had snapped off, like a patched-up handle on an old cup that had broken off again.

Grandad had to be hospitalized and have another operation, but he was still glad the repair had lasted for so many years, and he still talked about the accident itself with a fascination similar to the one we all had with the box of chocolates, mentioning the number of pieces and spreading his hands, who knew a foot could break into so many pieces, and that a box of chocolates could contain so many. Some were wrapped in shiny paper and had gooey liquor-like fillings, the taste of which never failed to surprise me.

At the end of the year there'd be leftover chocolates. Grandma would gather them up and put them in a bowl for the aunties and uncles who came to celebrate New Year with us. We'd spend it at Grandma and Grandad's because it would have been too difficult for them to travel home with me in the night, and Grandma would be a little absent then, her eyes not focused on me but on the door the guests would come in through, the glasses she'd fill, and all the food she'd prepared. I didn't like what she'd serve – shrimp cocktail or something else with shrimp and mayonnaise – and there was something about those New Year's Eves that made my stomach hurt. After dinner we would stand on the living room balcony and look out over the parking lot and the road to the shopping centre. There'd be a special tension in the air. They'd toast, and Grandad and the other old men would light sparklers and stick little rockets in the flower boxes and shoot them off, while Grandma and the aunties urged them to be careful. Fireworks lit up the cold black sky overhead, and I couldn't help but think how old the people standing around me were, that Grandma and Grandad would soon die, and that I was at the mercy of a force unknown to me.

My childhood continued long after it ended. Long after I became an adult, I continued to live like a child, and for a long time my childhood lived on in me. I couldn't let it go. I carried it with me, all the leaden images I had made of it, and in time I forgot many of the other things that also had been, so that the most striking recollections stood out even more.

I remembered an evening when I was home alone and once again sitting on the floor in the living room watching television and eating the pancakes my mother had made for me. When the children's programming ended, the news came on and, knowing they might show something I would wish I hadn't seen, I'd get up and change the channel, a program about rocks that I didn't want to see either. I turned off the television and quickly went to get a children's theatre LP with which I liked to fill the silence. I put the record on and lay down on the floor and listened. The songs were about war and the struggle for justice, I turned it over halfway through, and when the last song faded out I realized that it was already nightfall.

I got up and rushed to switch on all the lights. The rooms were tidy and still and the silence was palpable. When all the lights were shining, I ran into my mother's room and threw myself on the bed, where the undefined thing that lurked in the apartment when I was alone couldn't get me. I felt tiredness settle over me but also the anxiety biding its time somewhere inside me. I hadn't been able to undress and to brush my teeth because I knew it might spring to life then, so I lay under my mother's thick comforter just as I was, so I could drift off and into sleep. I wanted to fall asleep without noticing, because if I thought that's what I was doing, that sleep was coming to release me unto the morning, it became a struggle.

—

When morning came, I woke to find that I was still alone. It wasn't like being awakened by a sound or movement, not like her voice and body in the room. Instead, it was unseen and unheard. It was in the air that she hadn't come home, everything was different when she was there. This absence reached right in and had the strongest grip on me of all.

As I pulled off the covers and sat up in bed, I could hear my heart beating. It was strange. It wasn't fast but loud, incomprehensibly loud in a way that I'd never experienced before and that I couldn't imagine anyone else had experienced. How was it making that sound? I put my hands to my chest, but I could still hear the sound. Maybe there was nothing out of the ordinary about this, I thought. Maybe this was a thing that happened, only no one had told me about it. Maybe it was one of those things that was so obvious it wasn't discussed.

I placed my hand over my heart again as I got up and turned off the lights, trying to rid myself of this discomfort. It was bright outside, and on the living room floor the record sleeve was where I'd left it and next to it was my plate. I bent down and ran my finger through what was left of the melted sugar, stuck it in my mouth, and licked it off. My heart was beating even louder now, I felt like the sound might make me panic, and I did everything I could to stay calm. I wondered if I could die from this, or had I already? Was I dead? Could people hear their hearts when they died? That would explain why no one had told me about this, because maybe it wasn't the kind of thing to tell a child. The sun was shining above the rooftops and the industrial area and the rocky slope where our neighbour's things lay, a television and a telephone and more I couldn't discern. In the corner of the room the record was still spinning on my mother's gramophone. I lifted the little lever that regulated the arm with the needle, gently like she had taught me, and the moment I did, there was silence.

I looked at the record. Grey dust had gathered in the last groove where the needle had been. I wiped it away with my finger and went into the kitchen and opened the cupboard under the counter and dropped the dust into the garbage bag, and when I did, it was as if I could see myself from the outside. I saw myself from high above, as if I were God looking down at me moving around like a little ant in the kitchen, and I tried to lower my head and turn away so he couldn't see me. I opened the fridge and took out the light margarine and milk, and in the kitchen cupboard I found the bag of rallarhalvor. I looked at the picture and thought of the navvies as I took one out, carefully because they broke so easily.

Really only rye bread that was dark like this tasted good with a lot of butter. There was something about how the sourness stood in contrast to the fat, making its nauseating quality disappear. I spread it thick and was about to put the sandwich on the little tray my mother urged me to use, but changed my mind and put it right on the big white table without anything underneath. I didn't have to worry about what was important to her because she wasn't there anyway.

There was total silence, not even the buzz of the fridge could be heard. I sat down at the table and looked out at the thorn bushes and the morning sky over the trees in the park, took a bite of my sandwich and drank a sip of milk, but it tasted of nothing. I felt cold, as if a damp chill had entered me while I was asleep, and I wasn't hungry, but otherwise it wasn't much different than usual. It was just another morning. I usually ate breakfast alone, I thought, and I usually walked to school alone.

And when I thought about it, I knew she was safe and sound wherever she was, probably at his house. She simply hadn't come home. I wasn't worried anymore; on the contrary, I almost felt a little pleased that she wasn't there. That she had done something so wrong. A person who was so meticulous and who was also my mother. Not coming home in the evening was one thing, but staying away all night and not being there in the morning was really wrong, I was sure of it. It crossed some kind of line, I thought, and I was almost happy it had happened, because it gave me a reason to tell her how I felt about being left alone like this.

I got up from the table, threw out the sandwich, and put away the margarine and the bread and the milk, washed my glass, and wiped a few crumbs into the sink when I could have just as easily left them there. Then I gathered my things and got ready for school. I didn't need to get dressed, because I'd slept with my clothes on, and I wasn't going to wash or comb my hair or brush my teeth, but before I left, I checked to see that my pencil was in its place in my backpack, and I took the pencil sharpener out of its pocket and sharpened it to a point.

—

Outside the apartment door, I had to stand on my toes to reach the top lock and lock it like she'd taught me. I dared not ignore that rule. I walked out of the building, where the sun was glittering on the concrete and on the flagstone path along the bushes. I thought about what I would say to her, and with each step I took, it seemed as if I were approaching something conclusive. I hurried along the sidewalk so I could get to school. I wanted the hours to go by fast so the day would be over, and when she came home from work in the evening, I'd tell her what I was thinking and say everything I wanted to say to her.

Invariably I felt I had to escape the all-seeing eye that was following me, whether it was God's or my own. I walked faster, but as I was about to cross the street at the crosswalk, a taxi came to a stop right in front of me. The car door opened and her heeled boots hit the asphalt, she pushed the door shut behind her and walked up and hugged me and smiled and said my name. I felt everything else release its grip on me and I instantly softened, enveloped in her arms and in her scent. My mouth wanted to open and laugh and smile at her because she was home again. I couldn't be angry anymore, because now that she was right in front of me and holding me, it was almost as if I felt sorry for her.

But I kept my lips shut and stopped myself from smiling. I didn't say anything or hug her back.

I'll make amends for this, she said. She'd said this before, I didn't know that word, but I knew it meant we'd do something cozy, just her and me, when she got home from work that night, or on the weekend, or the weekend thereafter if it didn't happen sooner. She'd take me to the store to buy a tasty treat and we'd eat it together. I didn't say anything. I just nodded and tried not to look at her before turning away and moving on. I couldn't look at her and couldn't say any of the things I'd wanted to. I walked across the street and along the road that led away and down toward everything else, still with those eyes on me, burning into the back of my neck.

She'd always told me not to be sad when Grandma and Grandad died, but I couldn't understand how I was going to cope. For years, I braced myself. I shuddered at how it might feel and how lonely it would be for the one who was left behind.

But when it finally did happen, it took time. They didn't disappear from one day to the next, but gradually. Grandad went quieter and quieter and sat more and more still, and Grandma didn't really seem to be present anymore. They became a pair of shadows slowly fading before my eyes. The day my mother called to tell me he was dying, I took the train down and went into the old hospital and found him lying there, alone in a big room with only a bed and nothing more. I lay down beside him and held him in my arms. He felt so small and thin through the blanket they'd put around him, he was warm and breathing, but I wasn't sure he noticed me.

Grandma didn't talk much about him after he died, at least not with me. Maybe she didn't want me to be sad. She talked about other things, again and again she told me about the family she'd worked for when she was young, how nice they were, and about the time she went with the lady of the house to buy a hat. She told me about the prime minister she used to run into on the streetcar during that time and how friendly he was. It was as if those old memories were all that was left of her. She never cooked anymore, nor did she bake. Mom said she ate a lot of sweet things, as was often the case among very old people. Their sense of taste was dulled and so all they wanted was sweetness, but I hardly saw her eat anything. By and by, she was drawn away a little bit at a time, but it didn't feel like I thought it would, because I too had withdrawn from her life and into everything that had become mine. I hadn't had my daughter yet, but I was working a lot and often took long trips. And sometimes I travelled there and went up to the apartment and sat with her, but it wasn't as often as I'd imagined it would be.

When she didn't have long left, I'd visit her with my mother. The night before she died, we ate a prune soufflé because my mom said it was something I had to try, a true classic rarely seen on menus these days.

I don't remember which of us had the idea to go out for dinner, maybe I was the one who wanted to seize the opportunity, I liked it because it made me feel more grown-up and closer to her.

When the dessert arrived, she took the first bite and declared to me that it was perfect. She picked up the sauce boat and let the greyish-yellow cream spill over the soufflé. This is exactly as it should be, she said. She looked so beautiful in the light of the candelabras, at the table with the starched white tablecloth, and I wondered about all the previous occasions on which she'd been served a perfect prune soufflé.

—

I'd never eaten at a restaurant in the town where Grandma and Grandad lived. We'd visited the theatre-on-the-park together and the library and the swimming pool and the shopping centre, which smelled of plastic and rubber, and I was aware that there were restaurants of course, but it had never occurred to me to eat at one because they never did. But I knew they'd dined out after their wedding; sometimes my grandmother would retrieve the menu she'd saved along with other mementos and we'd look at it and laugh at what a wedding dinner cost in those days, a year or so before the war, at a place that later became a nightclub, which I'd been to many times.

My mother assured me they'd have thought it was good that we were indulging in a restaurant visit even though my grandmother was dying. At dawn the nursing home called and my mother arrived just in time to sit with her as she died. When I got there an hour later, the staff had lit a candle on the bedside table and put Grandma in a dress I'd never seen her wear. They'd cut it up the back and tucked it around her sides, as if to make her look a bit dressed up for an occasion.

In death, her face looked nothing like it did when she was alive. It was white and shapeless like the wheat dough she used to tip onto her pastry board, her skin was no longer smooth to my touch but floury, and her mouth was wide open.

It was her and yet not.

Her features had always been well-arranged, shaped by gentle laughter or an almost flirtatious expression, her mouth in a careful smile or closed around a morsel she'd just popped into it. Now her lips had fallen apart and her gaping mouth was a dark opening that made her face look like a man's. Grandad had looked like that when he slept on his back in the dinette, I'd looked into his open mouth every morning when I ran in and jumped on the sofa bed to wake him up. I'd never thought of Grandma as a woman who made an effort to be a certain way, but seeing her face like this made me think that death had revealed something inherent to her, but which she'd taken care to hide.

—

The staff had told my mother that one more piece of clothing would be needed when the body was transported and taken care of, so I brought one of the housecoats from my grandmother's closet, a dark blue one made of very thick polyester with red roses that resembled the party symbol she had everywhere. And when we went back to their apartment to go through their belongings, the first thing I did was reach for her apron. I took the clear green glass spice jars with the teak lids too, which they'd had in the kitchenette in the community garden cottage, and nickel-silver sugar tongs I'd never seen either of them use.

There was nothing special about that apron really, it was big and plaid, made of cotton, and not even particularly pretty. I lifted it off its hook, which was next to a wall hanging embroidered with the words *Coffee is the best of all earthly drinks*, I folded it up and put it in my bag. I'd been prepared and ready to let her go, still I wanted to hold on to something. An apron was tangible and useful. It was something I needed that I was sure no one else would want, like I knew no one would want the little crocheted potholders that also hung there, the copper stovetop covers, or the wooden stand with the scroll on which she wrote her shopping lists.

Overall there wasn't much in her kitchen or in their apartment that we, their children and grandchildren, wanted after they had died. Except for what Grandad had made, most of their furniture and things weren't the stuff people dreamed of inheriting. But when I held the apron in my hands, I could feel something sweet and warm enfold me and I could feel the fabric of her clothing and her body heat when she held me. How she had always held me. Her death was what would finally separate me from my childhood, I thought, the long beginning of a life I'd longed to get away from but couldn't seem to leave on my own.

~

When my father died, I was given his round wooden cutting board and the dark duckboard where he put his washed dishes. He used that oiled wooden board as a dish rack, aluminum fish pots as bread tins and old clay pots to hold his spatulas and whisks by his big stove. One time he'd made an enormous breakfast with my older brother, who had a different mother and lived far away from me but had spent more time with our father. The breakfast was for some guests who'd come to the summer house in the night, long after I'd gone to bed in the guest room. I had to help set the table and put out bottles of mineral water and beer from the large crate that was kept in a cool place; I did everything I could to do things right and comprehend all the instructions while studying my brother at work by the stove. On the gas flames were pans of fried eggs and white beans and grilled tomatoes and butter-fried mushrooms with garlic, and I noticed his irritation with the man who was giving orders, the man who was our shared father whom we knew in completely different ways, and I envied him it, how it bound them like rope no matter where they went in the kitchen and around the house.

~

I'd sliced bread on the cutting boards and put dishes to dry on the rack the last few times I'd visited. He'd moved to a house near the island he and my mother used to spend time on and it was as nice as the summer house. I took it as a gesture of great trust that I was allowed to navigate his kitchen, fetch the things he asked for, and do things when he ran out of time or couldn't do them himself. It felt as if he were inviting me into something I'd never before had access to, and that's how it was, and later being able to possess his things preserved that feeling for me after his death.

During our last visit, we ate lobster, and strangely enough it was the first lobster he'd ever made for me. He'd order from one of the fishermen he knew when I came to visit, but usually lobster was simply out of season, so it would be langoustines or maybe crab instead, even though crab was not considered a delicacy in the same way lobster was. When he stood in his kitchen and held the black animals, their tails flapping and wrenching in the air, I thought he was going to drive the knife into their heads and split them so as to fry them with the butter and herbs like my mother had said he'd do, but he just put them in a stock pot and left them to boil. He was skinny and his hair had thinned out. Several years had passed and I was an adult, but as usual I walked around like a child in his house, wondering what to say, whether to be quiet, how time would pass. And still I wondered who he was and how the two of us fit together.

—

My daughter was eight weeks old when he got to meet her for the first time. He was in town visiting an old friend, I met him with the stroller outside the market hall where he'd bought us shrimp sandwiches, and we went to his friend's house and ate them there. We drank white wine with them, which was as cold and good as the wine he drank always seemed to be, and I nursed and ate and nursed some more and spent a long time wondering if I should ask for more water. I still couldn't admit to being thirsty. He looked at my daughter when she was in my arms; showing her off to him felt strange, because the act also showed that I was his child. Had I not been, I would not have. He pronounced her name wrong and I pretended not to hear it.

After that, he kept suggesting I bring her with me when I came to visit, but I wanted to go alone. Keeping track of myself, with all it implied, was more than enough. I was no longer as afraid of getting a tension headache or a migraine and accidentally vomiting all over his dining table, but I couldn't be sure something like that wouldn't happen. I still couldn't trust my body.

—

As she grew older I'd bring her along to visit him when I couldn't think of an excuse not to. On one occasion two other guests were present as well, and as ever when he introduced me to the people he spent time with, or to anyone really, it made me feel chosen and flattered, all the while I worried about everything that could go wrong. One was a woman he was in a relationship with, who he'd known since his school days and who people said he'd probably always had relations with, and the other an assistant who helped him because he had become even weaker and had difficulty doing things as he was accustomed to. I don't remember the dinner but I remember the breakfast he'd laid out by the time we came down the next morning, or maybe he'd asked the others to lay out. Maybe, but it looked like he'd done it himself.

He stood in the middle of everything sparkling along with the table that had been laid. There was the Danish tea service and folded linen napkins at each plate, the large monogrammed ones I'd thought were kitchen towels, there were croissants and bread he'd ordered from the bakery on the quay. His usual strong lightly smoked tea wrapped everything in its vapours and he'd set out cheese and butter and marmalade in bowls and pots, toasted half the croissants and left the rest as they were, cut up dark rye bread and white rolls.

I tried to get my daughter to sit still next to me, but she kept sliding off her chair and darting off in his direction, trying to climb onto his lap or toward one of the many delicate and beautiful things in his home. I put her on my lap, but she slipped out of my grasp, and every time she got down on the floor I went after her, following her around to make sure she didn't break anything and to be able to pick her up quickly if she started crying or screaming or any of the other things a small child could suddenly start doing.

—

The last years with him flow together when I think about them. There was that salt-water-boiled lobster, and then there was the time in the middle of summer when he'd bought steaks to grill – although he rarely grilled, he made sure to point out, just like my mother and her boyfriend would when they grilled. Grilling wasn't really done, this was received knowledge, even if no one explained to me why. We simply didn't, like we didn't drink pop and eat fast food or watch a lot of TV or constantly say we loved each other. But now that he was older, my dad had put a big gas grill on the terrace. And I'd started to enjoy meat, right when everyone I knew had started talking about giving it up.

He cut fries to be cooked in the fryer, which he assured me was otherwise used only for squid, and tasked me with making the salad. He said nothing about what should be in it. I had a think and decided to make one like at the French restaurant where Grandad had worked as an errand boy, something I'd never told my father, even though he and I sometimes had lunch there when he was in the city where I lived. I moved around as carefully as ever in the kitchen, opened the fridge and beheld its contents, which looked so luxurious and at the same time hearty and somehow wholesome. In the vegetable drawer there was frisée and loose leaf lettuce, I took big pieces of the leaves, scallions that I sliced paper-thin, tomatoes I cut into thick even slabs, and I made a mustard vinaigrette with a lot of salt, which I mixed with a dollop of mayonnaise, so it would emulsify after shaking it to get that slightly creamy consistency. I picked chives from the herb garden he'd planted outside the door, snipped them over the salad, then spooned the dressing on top. While we were eating, he praised me for all of it: the chives, the dressing, and the fact that I'd cut the tomatoes in slices and not wedges, without him even having to ask me, as he said. Not many people know that tomatoes should be sliced in a salad like this, he said, looking at me, and I felt myself softening in his gaze, and the next day I called a friend to tell her that my dad had said I'd made a perfect salad.

I relayed this information as the great and amazing news it was to me, but she didn't seem nearly as happy for me as I'd expected her to be. He shouldn't care how you slice tomatoes, she hissed down the phone, and you shouldn't care what he thinks about it or anything else for that matter, she said.

I didn't understand why she was so annoyed.

—

A few days after his death, I made a large pot of cauliflower-and-millet soup that I imagined keeping in the fridge and taking out when I got hungry, which I assumed I'd be all the time, since I'd just had a baby. He had died right as my son was born. My mother had come to the hospital and told me I had a message on my voicemail that I needed to listen to, and when I did I heard the news of his death.

It was something I'd been thinking about my whole life or as long as I'd known of his existence. I'd always longed for his death, because I thought I could stop feeling shy and being afraid of him contacting me, but now that it had happened it felt so strange. Maybe it was the fact that I had almost called him the day before, I'd been standing in the little park outside our house with my cellphone in my hand and his number on the screen, but I hadn't dared and told myself it was better to call after the child was born.

I had also always imagined that he would call me before he died and offer me an explanation, as I'd seen fathers do in the movies. But he hadn't even told me he was sick again. Maybe there was nothing to explain, after all.

—

His passing came as a relief. I wouldn't have to bring another child into a familial relationship that I had such a hard time maintaining. I sat at the big white table thinking this, gulping down the millet soup I'd warmed only slightly to be on the safe side, while the baby in my arms drew milk into itself and I told myself again that my father's death was a good thing. But my cheeks were burning with all the embarrassment and disappointment I was feeling for not having been told. A dull ache was pressing on my temples, and when I'd almost emptied the entire bowl of lukewarm white soup, my ears began to ring and nausea welled up inside me.

I pried my breast out of the little mouth that had such a powerful hold on it and got up from the table before I'd even tucked it back into my clothes. I burped my son and put him down in his little bed and noticed the room was spinning. The walls and the whole apartment were spinning and the floor seemed to fall away from under my feet. I collapsed and crawled to the bed and pulled myself into it and then stood on all fours among the covers and sheets and vomited. The soup I had cooked to cope with everything came out of me with such an unexpected force, it sprayed out of my mouth and all over the bed and the wall behind it.

I sometimes think of his voice, to remember how it sounded, and of his face, so as to forever remember what it looked like. He left me nothing, but my brother made sure I got what I wanted of all that was in his home.

There was so much there that I liked. I took an oblong fish kettle in which he'd stored bread, something I'd never seen in anyone else's house; a turbot kettle for large loaves; and a pike kettle for baguettes. In a much smaller kitchen like mine, the kettle was large and unwieldy, but having it there and knowing how he'd used it made me feel like I was someone who'd been close to him, like he was my father.

I put all the bread I baked in my kettle, I liked making good bread and putting it in there, as well as organizing everything else I had in the kitchen and finding the best places for it. I wanted it to look nice, but I also wanted everything to stay as fresh as possible, so that I would never have to throw away anything that could be put to use. I hung a braid of garlic on the wall like Grandma's, put avocado in one bowl, fruit in another, leafy vegetables in the warmer part of the fridge, and lacto-fermented carrots and sauerkraut and kimchi in big glass jars at the top.

After having more children and not working as much as before, I spent even more time in the kitchen. I was constantly thinking of new dishes and ingredients to prepare. I wanted to teach the children to enjoy good food that I cooked according to the rules of the art without simplifications or skipping any steps, I wanted everything they ate to nourish their growing little bodies, and I wanted us to sit down at the big white table and eat together so they wouldn't turn out like me. I let them taste oysters and homemade liver paté and Christmas food and herring, I made stocks and broths and ossobuco and saffron risotto and roast beef and Vietnamese spring rolls and pho and fried dumplings and fish cakes and homemade corn tortillas for tacos, and when we just wanted something simple, I made platters of herbed chicken and oven-roasted vegetables.

Invariably, I was in the kitchen. I went in there to devote myself to an essential task that I enjoyed and that we all needed, but it was as if I got stuck in there and ever more often I'd eat what I cooked on my own when it was ready because I was so hungry and couldn't wait. I didn't even put it on a plate or sit down; I stood at the stove or kitchen counter, staring at the shiny white tiles, eating directly from the pot with the ladle or my bare hands, while my husband and children were in the next room occupied with something else.

Those times it was as if hunger assailed me. I think it was the shock of having given birth to three children of whom I was the mother and who would grow up and have their own lives, live and die like everyone else, and maybe even have their own children. It filled me with fear and wonder, and to think only of what they would get to eat and how I could give them the best I could manage was so calming and pleasant.

It was unreal to be in possession of all those things I thought I never was meant to have. An existence that seemed simple and was so full of life. I had enough money to buy whatever I wanted in the stores in our neighbourhood, where locally grown vegetables were neatly arranged and there were nitrite-free artisanal sausages, free-range eggs, and cheeses made in small dairies far out in the archipelago. I could go to farms outside the city and buy meat and suet with which to render thick white frying fat that I remembered my grandmother making once when I was there, and I had time to bake overnight-proofed cinnamon buns that were twice the size of hers and look for recipes for healthy little nibbles and snacks that were fun to make for the kids or with them. All the while I reminded myself how grateful I should to be for all this.

—

I loved food and how it made my life real, but I was still afraid of it. I was afraid of everything I did with it and everything I felt it was threatening to do to me. I no longer threw up, but I made sure to eat only what I thought was healthy to compensate for the amount I was eating. I wished I could stop keeping myself in check, but unless I did, there was no limit to how much I could devour. Suddenly I'd find myself eating a whole tray of seeded crisp bread or kale chips.

I was thinking ever more often about how to make this stop, but also about what I could eat that wouldn't trigger my compulsive eating. According to psychoanalysis, compulsive overeaters tend to get stuck in an antagonistic relationship with the food they want and put as much energy into what to eat and not eat as a junkie does into getting drugs. That's pretty much how I perceived what I was doing, and when it was clear that this fear and obsession would not leave me, I realized that I could try to force myself out of the kitchen by getting my husband to do the cooking instead. This was a new approach for me – figuring out what I needed and asking another person for it – and I never imagined it could be that simple.

They say memory is linked to language and language is what allows a young child to create memories. My mother and my grandmother used to tell me that I'd said all the usual words children say when they're learning to talk, like *look* and *lamp* and *mama* – so *Schwarzwald* was not the first thing to come out of my mouth, but they talked about it so often I seemed to remember the very feeling of saying that word for the first time.

I had just turned one, a birthday party was being held at the home of one of my mother's friends, and someone had ordered a cake from a bakery in the city. It was in a white box tied with white string, it was a Schwarzwald cake, my mother had said. Schwarzwald, she said again when I was sitting on her lap and the cake was placed in front of us. I'd never seen anything like it and had never known that such a thing as cake existed. White garlands of icing piped close together, delicate dark chocolate flakes around the sides, a sprinkling of shaved milk chocolate on top, and in the middle of it all a pink rose was in bloom, plump and moist.

I remember her repeating the word slowly and me trying to repeat it while looking at her face very close to mine. I wanted to say it again and again. The sounds and syllables moved around and around in my mouth, diverging from everything I'd known until then with the same improbable exquisiteness as the cake itself. They'd bought it for my sake, but it seemed to delight them as well. Mom showed me how to hold my spoon, but when I got it into my mouth and felt the cream on my tongue, my mouth opened again as if of its own accord, and when they took a little piece of the rose and gave it to me, the same thing happened.

A one-year-old's birthday party with a cake from a pastry shop doesn't fit with the image I have of how we lived then, and it doesn't align with what I think I know about the people who were my mother's friends. But I know it's true because there's a photo of me sitting next to the cake with a few of her friends' children. Actually, it might be the photograph I'm remembering. In the years that followed, I saw it as often as I heard the story of how I'd spoken the name of the cake when I was only one year old.

Schwarzwald. Svartskogen, the black forest.

Nowadays I could bake a cake like that myself if I wanted to, but such a thought would never have occurred to any of the women at my birthday party, not my mother or any of her friends. They didn't do that kind of thing nor did they do anything else that took time in the kitchen, at least not like I've done throughout my life ever since then. On the contrary, they'd put as much distance between them and the kitchen as they could. Food and cooking seemed to mean nothing to them, and I have often wished I was more like them.

—

I started baking cakes around when I was supposed to be spending less time in the kitchen. It provided an outlet for a need similar to cooking, but did not overwhelm my existence in the same way because there weren't as many opportunities to bake a cake as there had been to cook food. I'd been given a cookbook on cakes, with a number of Italian recipes that used soft cheeses such as ricotta and mascarpone instead of cream. I read everything in the book and followed all the instructions, learning how to lay out the mise en place for cake baking and how to plan their making, how to beat the eggs for the batter long enough to get fluffy bottoms, and how to cut layers with a really sharp knife and level it where necessary, measuring out the fillings for the different layers in exact amounts and spackling the cake once before icing it, so that no crumbs from the cake base would find their way to the surface.

I baked macarons that were left to set on trays on our warm bathroom floor and garnished my cakes with them, I got food colouring to turn the cake fillings different hues, ordered American cake candles that were narrow and tall, and piped different patterns right on the kitchen counter to learn how to get the flare and the exact right angle with the nozzle. I folded marzipan roses, bought palette knives and tall cake platters and special spikes you stuck into the cake so you could decorate it with fresh flowers, whether or not they were edible.

As soon as a birthday or any other good occasion was in the offing, I started planning. I loved figuring out what I was going to do and allowing myself to be consumed by it for days and then standing alone at the kitchen counter and running my long palette knife over different types of frostings and glazes again and again until the cake was smooth. It demanded my full attention and all my time, made me let go of everything to which I otherwise devoted myself, and I hardly knew what that was so long as I was standing there.

I could think of nothing else when baking cakes and could feel nothing more than the intoxicating anticipation that presented itself each time. I loved the preparations, the care, and the meticulous work, but also the way everyone would look at the cake when it was finished and how it got eaten up and disappeared in an instant, and I also loved the unnecessary nature of it all. How the production of a magnificent cake was kind of the opposite of cooking, because it was never really needed and not expected, least of all from someone like me, who was probably thought to have better things to do. Or was I the only one who thought so – that I should be devoting myself to something more important, whether I liked it or not.

~

As I remember it, there was Schwarzwald cake on my birthday for several years, not because I wanted to eat it, but because of the name, because my mother and I liked saying it like I'd said it when I was only one year old. That first one was probably the only one that was store-bought, and the cakes Grandma made every subsequent year were probably her own variations. Reading my cake book, I realized that a Schwarzwälder Kirschtorte, named after the Black Forest mountain range in southwest Germany and also called Schwarzwald cake, was made in a different way. It consists of dark chocolate bases soaked in cherry liqueur and covered with preserved cherries and cream, and I decided to make one for my mother on her seventieth birthday. It took several days to get it ready, which was exactly what I wanted. I bought large amounts of mascarpone and a packet of extra-fine cocoa, cherry liqueur, the classic one made from the same recipe for over a century because I thought she would appreciate it, that she might actually be able to taste that it was this particular kind – and cherries that I pitted and put in my own brine so they wouldn't be too sweet, because I knew she wouldn't like it if they were.

I still knew what she liked, but I hadn't yet begun to think that my own children might relate to me in the same way, be equally as keen to fulfill my unspoken wishes as they imagined them. I baked the bases with the cocoa and bought a special baking chocolate from Valrhona, from which I assembled a thick and shiny ganache that ended up with precisely the right depth and richness, perfect for her, I thought, and the night before the party I assembled the cake so that it would set and be stable enough to transport by taxi, but also so that the flavours would stand out better, the bitter and the sweet hand in hand.

I emptied our fridge and rearranged it so the cake would fit inside along with the other one I'd baked, which was the same size, and on the day of the party I garnished it with a couple of handfuls of fresh cherries and more chocolate ganache that I let spill over the edges. And no cream of course. For a party with people of my own age, I probably wouldn't have dared make a real Schwarzwald cake, because the allure of the sweet boozy tang of preserved cherries together with the rich, heavy chocolate was probably an acquired taste, but like most such tastes, it became all the more enticing once you started to enjoy it.

So it was with everything. But to be on the safe side, I'd made an alternate, a caramel cake with dulce de leche, which involved a process that I find endlessly entertaining – taking a can of condensed milk and letting it sit for three hours in a pot of simmering water and then opening it up to reveal a thick, caramelized sauce. The caramel cake was much less demanding, easier for everyone to enjoy, semi-sweet and fluffy with a milkier chocolate buttercream blended with mascarpone and flavoured with espresso and a few pinches of salt flakes sprinkled on top. The cakes would complement each other nicely, I thought. They were ample in circumference, but also tall; I'd used regular round springform pans and made double the amount of both bases and fillings, so that it wouldn't matter if one was more popular than the other.

—

It was a big party with lots of guests, and I wanted there to be more than enough for everyone. I don't remember if I'd cooked the food for the occasion as well: I often offered to because I liked doing it so much – putting together a menu and cooking lots of food for many people – but whenever I did, I also became a bit suspicious of my motives.

When I received praise for my dishes, I felt like a child again sitting at a party or under a table at one of my mother's and her friends' regular haunts, waiting for someone to say something about me or to me, or to ask to see what I'd drawn or written. Those adults were by and large the same ones who were her friends now, and they were almost as exuberant and mysterious as I thought they were back then, with their boisterous discussions about politics and all sorts of things. But they were also friendly and interested. They'd come into the kitchen and thank me for the food, eager to discuss something they wanted my opinion on, and I couldn't help thinking how anti-social I was for preferring to be in there rather than joining the party. But the pleasure and satisfaction outweighed my sense of shame, my need for validation, and my inability to accept praise.

I don't think I reflected on the fact that giving her an authentic Schwarzwald cake –one I'd baked myself to boot – was a way of reconnecting with the past. Nor did I think about what it meant that I wouldn't taste even a crumb of it, I was only thinking about the cake in relation to how it would taste, that I wouldn't be able to sample it, but you can't really sample a cake unless you do test bakes to try out various versions. You have to trust the recipe and your intuition, which I liked. The uncertainty attracted me, having put in so much work but not being able to be sure that it really was good.

And even if I had tasted it, I probably wouldn't have been able to judge it. After all, I'd never liked cake, and my own sense of sweetness was compromised because I no longer ate anything sweet. Because I found it so difficult to stop when I started, it felt easier to stop completely, and I imagined I felt better for it. I wondered if anyone would notice that I wasn't having a piece myself and what I would say if someone asked. I didn't want them to think I was on a diet or that I had a disordered relationship with food either, and from what I'd read about eating disorders, I knew that something like baking for others but not eating yourself was classified as disordered eating.

—

When I took the cakes from the counter, where they'd been left to warm to room temperature after all their hours in the fridge, and carried them to the buffet table, where everything else had been eaten up and put away, one of the younger guests came over. She stood in front of the cakes with wide eyes, asking questions about what was in them and how I'd made them. It was probably normal, unproblematic curiosity, like children are curious about everything sweet because it's yummy or about baking and cooking because it's fun and because these activities have become a kind of natural pastime for children as well. At least in families who can afford to waste food if it gets ruined.

But the thought that she might be like me also flitted by. I'd always been so convinced that no one could be, and even after I started talking to others who'd struggled with food, I decided that I wasn't like them, no matter how much I resonated with what they told me about how they ate and thought about eating. They told me this was also a sign – one of the things that characterizes an addict is the feeling of not being like other people and that what is common knowledge does not apply to you.

They told me that recovery was like peeling an onion. It was a metaphor to which they kept returning. None of them seemed to care how hackneyed it was, none seemed afraid of saying what had already been said so many times before, and I've noticed that I've become like that myself. I've often told others that it's how it is – we continue to uncover new layers in ourselves.

For a long time I thought I'd turned to them after I made the rice pudding. In my mind, that evening and night were like a boundary, even though it took me a while to grasp what had actually happened. I felt ashamed that I'd been so angry with my daughter for not tasting the food I'd prepared for us, but the worst part was how the shame rendered me even more inadequate.

It laid bare everything I couldn't do or say and this shocked me. I'd been prepared for the fact that having a child would be difficult, but never would I have imagined that I'd be unable to show my child all the love I felt.

—

In my mind, the rice pudding episode was the critical event that led me to ask for help. It's possible that all this speaks to is an individual's need for critical events when trying to understand themselves, about the longing for a clear beginning and an end to a story such as this one, but it could also be that it really was the beginning, it's just that it took such a long time. In the introduction to a proven self-help program for compulsive eating disorders, it states that it takes an average of ten years for a person with abnormal eating behaviours to seek help, and I don't know from when the psychologist who formulated this starts counting, but for me it did indeed take very many years.

I'd found my way out of the kitchen and I'd stopped binge eating and vomiting by the time I turned to them – support groups and addiction therapists and their discussions and meetings – but I was still stuck inside myself and still afraid of food. I was afraid I'd sink even deeper than I'd sunk that night and would continue to abandon my children the way I was doing then. I was afraid they too would start using food as an escape in the way I did and that I'd choose it over them, like an alcoholic who chooses the bottle.

The people I started calling when I needed to talk were strangers. I didn't know their names or anything else about them, but they said I could contact them whenever I wanted, and our conversations followed certain scripts that made it easy to get close to each other. It was freeing to answer their questions and hear them talk about how they themselves had eaten and behaved with food. Before that, I'd never have been able to say a word about this. If I ever managed to open my mouth and get something out, it was – as it so often is – with what's difficult or almost unbearable; I'd only get a tiny bit out, and that tiny bit was far too easy to overlook and misinterpret.

It's hard to listen to what you don't want to hear and it's hard to listen to someone who doesn't actually want to speak. Moreover I was also a person who'd never talked much, and certainly not about my many weaknesses and the many things I couldn't do. They taught me how to express all that and to talk about the importance of food in my life, but even after I got used to it, it turned out to be quite difficult to talk about it with people in what I considered to be the ordinary world, those who were not addicts of any kind or who identified as such.

I'd despised myself for not having the courage to speak, but when I started being forthright about certain topics, I realized it wasn't quite as rewarding as I'd imagined it would be. It wasn't as if everyone around me had been going around waiting for me to open my mouth, and it wasn't as if everyone understood, or wanted to try to understand, what I was talking about when I was talking about food.

In all likelihood I wasn't alone in having strong emotions bound up with eating, I thought, and perhaps I was not as alone in having difficulties with it as I imagined. Some people got annoyed and told me I shouldn't problematize something as natural as food and eating, hunger and pleasure, and someone explained that I couldn't possibly have any such problems because I didn't have a weight issue. Others explained to me that all women more or less had an eating disorder, society as a whole had an eating disorder, and it was part of being a woman to have a disturbed relationship to food, to your own body and your desires. It wasn't a big deal and it wasn't unique to me, but something I should learn to live with. I'd never thought of it that way.

—

But do you see it as an addiction or an eating disorder? one of my friends asked. I said that I saw it as an eating disorder, though this wasn't true. At the time, I was thinking of it as an addiction, but I didn't dare admit as much to anyone outside of the addiction world, as the idea of food or sugar addiction was only an idea and not an established diagnosis.

Nonetheless this question preoccupied me too, not least because I wanted to know what to do to get rid of my problem once and for all. Now it no longer matters, it is no longer as important to understand it through this lens, but at the time I dwelled on it and on my misgivings about the fact that I was thinking about all this in the first place. Had I blown everything out of proportion? Not being able to stop yourself from eating too much was a luxury problem, and when I sought help from mainstream health care, I was informed that I did not have an eating disorder.

That said, I didn't feel addicted in the way that many of the people I spoke to seemed to be, those who suffered severe psychological or social consequences because of their boundless eating, who'd stolen food or money for food and become morbidly obese. I found myself wishing that I was like them, envying them their apparent sense of clarity, but also the food orgies I imagined they still indulged in. In my secret fantasies, they enjoyed food without restraint and at liberty, as if they were of a different kind and didn't care about any of what I cared about.

None of them had loved food as I still did, in spite of everything. They spoke of food as fuel or a mental obsession, and notions that it had intrinsic value or could tell us about the world and our place in it were interpreted as yet another expression of morbid obsession. But at the same time, they argued that such disinterest was part of what had led them into this disease. The problem for them had never been that they loved to cook and eat food, they said, but that they loved to eat what they believed was manufactured by the food industry precisely to make people addicted.

Upon hearing this, again I mourned not having been able to devote myself to what I truly wanted. I wondered if my friends had perhaps been right, the ones who'd told me how wonderful it was, wasn't it?, that I liked cooking and other domesticities so much, that they would have liked to have a smidgen of that disposition themselves and that they wished I could just allow myself to give in to it, if that's what I wanted so badly. Was the inability to take pleasure in fact the greatest sin and was my problem my seeking of faults in myself, and my own notions of the person I thought I should be? Perhaps my darkness and my failings were universal, only that others didn't allow themselves to be governed by them as I had. Why couldn't I have stayed in the light instead of forever being drawn into the dark?

They've told me I have to find a way to step outside of this if I'm going to talk about it. I have to visualize it as something I can walk into and out of, and I try to do as they say.

I see before me a forest.

A black forest with a path leading into the trees and I'm following it while holding something in my hand that will help me find my way out again. White pebbles, like in the tale of the children who went into the forest and were captured by the witch after they started eating her house. A spotlight, the light of which illuminates the darkness inside. A long rope that I tie to one of the trees at the start of the path.

I haven't taken the time to think those thoughts through, and so I wonder if it's because I don't want to step outside. Do I want to go back into it and never come out again? Might I actually be longing to enter the darkness, despite everything I know about it? Is that what the addiction is – walking straight into a familiar dark without giving a thought to the risks? Knowing all about loneliness and choosing it nonetheless?

I wonder if I want to use storytelling as an excuse to step inside again. I think of all the other things I'd rather open myself up to. Could this be what it means to recover – opening oneself up to all that has been lost and all that is on its way out?

—

For a while I thought this was about becoming a better person. But then one of them told me that she also thought along these lines but had now realized the fallacy of it.

It's about becoming a human being, she said.

Weren't we already?

We were of course human beings like everyone else, it was just that we didn't really know what it meant. At least I had never known, and I needed them so I could learn.

It was a while before I could take up cooking again, and I no longer do it in the same way as before. I peel onions and garlic and try to exist in this world.

We don't talk as often now, but sometimes I'll call one of them to ask how it's all going and maybe tell them about something new I've learned. Or that I'm not as frightened or lonely anymore and that I have a different perspective now.

And if I do, I can be sure I'll be hearing the onion analogy again. Many people say they don't really like to think of themselves as an onion because of its structure, that there's nothing at the heart of it, and my reply is that I don't mind. It doesn't scare me. On the contrary, I like the idea of an emptiness deep inside. I imagine it as a big white void that I can fall right into.